Preserving Eden

The Nature Conservancy

Text by Noel Grove

Photographs by Stephen J. Krasemann

Harry N. Abrams, Inc. Publishers, New York

Page 1: *A hoary marmot on Mt. Ranier snacks on Indian paintbrush, part of the summer fare the animal uses to put on fat for winter hibernation.*

Pages 2–3: *Shallows of the Platte River in Nebraska afford migrating sandhill cranes a welcome stopover on their way to breeding grounds in Canada and Alaska. Some 10,000 acres of this critical area are protected by The Nature Conservancy in cooperation with other groups.*

Page 5: *The American avocet frequents both salty and freshwater shorelines.*

Pages 6–7: *Sunset lights the rim of Aravaipa Canyon in Arizona, a desert habitat now protected by The Nature Conservancy after its purchase by Defenders of Wildlife.*

Pages 8–9: *A bison grazes safely on the Samuel H. Ordway, Jr. Memorial Prairie Preserve in South Dakota.*

Page 10: *False dragonhead blooms among shoreline grasses of the fabled Suwannee River, object of Nature Conservancy protection efforts since the late 1970s.*

Page 11: *Wild impatiens blooms near a waterfall in TNC-supported La Selva Research Station in Costa Rica.*

Pages 12–13: *A mountain lion kitten looks out on an uncertain future, where hunting still threatens.*

Pages 14–15: *Dolphins leap in tandem in Florida waters, where Conservancy efforts helped persuade Federal officials to greatly expand the National Marine Sanctuary.*

Page 16: *Dawn and dew show off a spider's artwork.*

Page 17: *Squirrel tail, or wild barley, brushes the air in a midwestern meadow. When dry, the seeds scatter as their bristles attach to the fur of animals.*

EDITOR: Robert Morton

DESIGNER: Dana Sloan

Library of Congress Cataloging-in-Publication Data
Krasemann, Stephen J.
The nature conservancy: preserving Eden/
    photographs by Stephen Krasemann; text by Noel Grove.
p.   cm.
ISBN 0-8109-3663-1
1. Nature Conservancy (U.S.)—History.
2. Nature conservation—United States—History.
3. Natural areas—United States—History.
I. Grove, Noel.
QH76.K73   1992
333.95'16'06073—dc20   91-24551
                              CIP

Contents

"Nothing Should Become Extinct"

For centuries the sharp bite of late autumn prodded grizzly bears of the great plains up the spires of the Rocky Mountain front. In the packed snow of wind-blasted slopes they clawed out dens and slept away the winter. Fat and sluggish from a diet of berries and pine nuts when they entered, they were lean engines of fury, ignited by hunger, when they emerged in spring. Months of abstinence had gnawed to the edge of their flesh and it was flesh they craved to make up the loss. Any living animal in their path, including their smaller kin the black bear, could be smacked down and devoured if caught.

At its best behavior, *Ursus arctos horribilis* is a monarch commanding total respect in North American wildlands. The bunched mass of its body topped by a muscular hump suggests power even as it ambles along in a puppy-dog walk, broad head swinging from side to side. At full speed its cinnamon coat quivers and jerks in all directions, as if demons beneath are goading it into unstoppable motion.

Explorers Lewis and Clark described their first grizzlies with awe: "a verry large and turrible looking animal which we found verry hard to kill..." Kill them they did, whenever possible, before measuring forearms nearly two feet in circumference. "The largest of the carnivorous kind I ever saw," wrote Clark, not realizing that grizzlies spend most of their waking moments browsing on plants and insects.

Fortunately, during their carnivorous appetite in spring, sustenance often awaited them in cool storage. Emerging from the snow were carcasses of elk, deer, and bison that had failed to survive the long winter. Desperate hunger abated, the bears took up residence in the lowlands, munching on salads of cow parsnip and angelica, sometimes even grazing placidly within sight of hoofed neighbors.

Eventually a new and very different neighbor stepped into the annual routine of the grizzly bear and changed life on the great plains forever. People came, creating ranches and towns and replacing the elk and buffalo with cattle. The voracious beast of uncertain temperament and awesome weaponry found little place in their lives and was no match for repeating rifles, traps, and poison. The ambling monarch became the trespasser, feared and unwanted.

Although population estimates in Alaska range up to 42,000, by 1991 only 700–900 grizzlies survived in the lower states of Wyoming, Idaho, Washington State, and Montana. Especially at the point where the western mountains meet the midcontinental prairie they seemed destined for disappearance, until a domain was set aside where the great bear remains king.

In 1978 an organization called The Nature Conservancy bought the first of 18,000 acres of prime grizzly habitat on the eastern front of the Rockies. The property now known as Pine Butte Swamp Preserve begins in meadows and willow thickets of the plains of western Montana, climbs rounded foothills covered with limberpine and aspen, and leads to steep crags owned by the United States government's Bureau of Land Management. The Conservancy and BLM properties plus land owned by the Montana Fish and Game Department total some 40,000 acres of prime grizzly country.

The shrunken realm of the western grizzly is a dramatic and perhaps overstated example of what is happening to millions of species on this planet. In the environmental renaissance of the 1990s, millions of people fret over the possible disappearance of the grizzly bear. Most of them may not realize that setting aside a block of woods to save it does not fit the mountain-prairie routine of old silvertip, whose lowland haunts are now coveted by farmers and ranchers. Salvation for the largest carnivore in North America requires plucking out a sizable piece of the bear's original home and leaving it intact. So it is with millions of species—most of them much less imposing than the grizzly—that are being crowded off this planet.

Now dominant on the earth after thousands of years as an intelligent but somewhat puny resident, we of Homo sapiens have proven ourselves poor stewards. Squandering our inheritance before it has been fully appraised, we wipe out species at random without even knowing how many species exist. Estimates of the total plants and animals that share space with us range from five million to thirty million. At present rates of destruction, a quarter of them may be gone in the next twenty-five years.

As the numbers of other species plummet, our own is on an astronomical rise. It took Homo sapiens thousands of years to reach a population at the birth of Christ that was less than that of the United States today. By 1800 we had reached our first billion—today's China—scattered over the globe. In the next 200 years as sanitation improved and diseases were conquered, our numbers shot to five billion. In the explosive multiples of reproductivity, that number could double in the next fifty years even if the entire world achieved zero population birth rates, unlikely soon.

In the previous century and early in this one, animals such as the grizzly, wolf, cougar, bobcat, and coyote were called "varmints" and executed on sight. Smaller animals were assumed to be inexhaustible and any plants beyond those of practical use were beyond consideration.

OVERLEAF:
Ecologists employed by The Nature Conservancy scout Pine Butte Preserve in Montana for signs of grizzly bears.

By the twentieth century we had realized our capabilities for destruction. Passenger pigeons once flew over America in flocks so huge they blotted out the sun as they passed overhead and broke down trees when they came to roost. Hunting brought those hordes down to one bird, which died alone in a cage in 1914. When settlers began moving west the total weight of bison—perhaps sixty million—in this country once far exceeded the weight of our current human population. By 1889 they numbered less than 600 animals. The oceans were not big enough to hide the right whale, so right for whalers that they harpooned it nearly to extinction.

Before the turn of the present century so many voices were raised in protest that the environmental movement was born. The Audubon Society was founded in 1886, the first major environmental group. Chapters of the organization dedicated to preventing extinctions of birds by plume hunters spread nationwide and influenced the passage of bird protection laws in thirty-two states. Theodore Roosevelt observed of the bison reduction, "Never before . . . were so many large wild animals of one species slain in so short a space of time" and he called conservation . . . "the most weighty question now before the people of the United States." During his eight years as president 230 million acres were set aside as public land, protection much influenced by his friend John Muir, founder of the Sierra Club.

Today it is not hunting that threatens large numbers of species so much as our own proliferation. We crowd out species by changing their habitat to create croplands and grazing, cities and superhighways. In the process we pollute their homes, introduce new predators, and trap them in islands of vegetation from which they find no migratory escape.

Ecology was a word familiar to few but scientists at the start of this century, but a group of them formed the Ecological Society of America. Even then, members recognized that virgin America was disappearing under the axe and the plow, its air becoming tainted by fossil fuel emissions.

In 1917 a study group was formed within the Ecological Society called the Committee for the Preservation of Natural Conditions. For almost three decades the group held intellectual discussions about deteriorating ecosystems, verbal exercises that eventually proved unsatisfying to some members of the committee. In 1946 the dissidents split with the Ecological Society to form a separate organization called The Ecologist's Union, a well-advised move perhaps, except for the name. The word "union" has rarely been known to spur philanthropy from the wealthy, and the group sputtered along on dues and small donations from its thousand or so members.

During those early years, one of the members, an urbane engineer and conservationist named Dick Pough, traveled to England and learned of the work of the British government's Nature Conservancy, which set aside land for open space and wildlife preserves. Upon returning to the U.S. he urged the Union to adopt the same goal and even the same name, but recommended that it stay private and seek charitable donations instead of depending on government budgets. Pough had connections as well as imagination and after The Ecologist's Union changed its name to The Nature Conservancy (TNC) in 1951 he began tapping his wealthy acquaintances. Mrs. DeWitt Wallace, co-founder and co-owner of The Reader's Digest, gave $100,000. Pough's friend Katharine Ordway, a Minnesota mining heiress, steered $53 million into Conservancy work.

The group began buying natural areas and accepting donated sites. That often meant land too steep to build on or too wet to farm—little-used, inexpensive properties that prompted one observer to call the early Conservancy a "gully and hemlock society."

TNC's first purchase in 1955 fitted the description. It was Mianus Gorge,

A burrowing owl holds a grasshopper in its talons. Despite its name, this diminishing species does not dig its own hole but uses the dens of badgers and prairie dogs. Cultivation of prairie habitats reduces such opportunities.

sixty acres of stately hemlocks along the steep-sided Mianus River an hour north of New York City. Available and relatively inexpensive, it was about to be swallowed in the postwar building boom. Today it is a quiet, lovely poet's park, now expanded to 560 acres. A path on the preserve guides visitors along the modest stream that spills over boulders and flows under fallen tree trunks.

Another early project was a bog called the Sunken Forest on Fire Island, a popular vacation spot near New York City on the south shore of Long Island. One of the early presidents of the organization, Richard Goodwin, offered his small meadow and woodlands in Connecticut, which became Burnham Brook Preserve. It provided space where a few naturalists could net butterflies, identify birds, and name plants. The Nature Conservancy was acquiring and preserving land, but so were others. The federal wildlife refuge system was expanding. The Audubon Society was establishing its own private preserves, and in fact resented the Conservancy's competition for donations.

By the 1970s, with the acquiring and managing of real estate now a major part of its activities, the earlier scientific personality of the Conservancy had taken on the look of business. The vague drift into property collection bothered some of its leaders, including one young, energetic employee named Pat Noonan who had a masters degree in business administration as well as city and regional planning. Noonan combined a love of the outdoors with a passion for planning and business. He wanted an organization with a precise purpose, not just one that amassed land at random, and in the Conservancy's cramped office in downtown Washington, D.C. he gathered other bright, young business minds around him with similar inclinations. For months they met over beers in nighttime workshops to determine the character and personality of The Nature Conservancy, something that would distinguish it from other environmental groups.

OPPOSITE, ABOVE:
A bighorn ram plunges down a snowy slope at the Eastern Front of the Rockies. In the bitter Montana winter bighorn sheep come down to the shelter of trees in Pine Butte Preserve.

OPPOSITE, BELOW:
Ear Mountain, named for the shape of its rocky summit, stands out in the million-acre Bob Marshall Wilderness in Montana. Adjoining TNC's Pine Butte Swamp Preserve, the huge unspoiled area offers a wide range to animals using TNC's combination of mountain and prairie habitats.

OVERLEAF:
The last towering wrinkles of the Eastern Front of the Rocky Mountains are mirrored in a small lake where the range gives way to prairie. The junctions of two ecosystems are often rich in species that take advantage of both types of habitat.

The key was handed them by the lone scientist on the staff, a big, red-haired biologist named Bob Jenkins. Now science director of TNC, Jenkins suggested saving only lands of certain ecological worth, not just acquiring properties because they appeared "natural" and undisturbed. He insisted that biotic diversity must be maintained on this planet and said the Conservancy should establish gene pools, not only of species but sub-species and unique biological communities. Nothing, preached Jenkins with messianic zeal, should become extinct.

This was strong fare in the early 1970s. The idea of extinctions was then generally understood to mean the dodo, the passenger pigeon, and the passing of the dinosaurs, with more current concern for the Bengal tiger and the giant panda. Jenkins was suggesting an unprecedented campaign to rescue any species, no matter how obscure or seemingly worthless. Clear to him but not to others was the importance of genetic variation, the idea that the hidden strengths of one living thing may benefit another. The sessions often became loud arguments between those who felt the Conservancy should protect any land it could get its hands on, and Jenkins, who would restrict acquisitions to land containing plants or animals in danger of disappearing.

In the end, the clarity of purpose in Jenkins' proposal appealed to the business minds. After months of soul-searching, objectives began to emerge. The Nature Conservancy would henceforth seek out and attempt to save species and biotic communities that stood in danger of disappearing under human pressures. It would buy the land when necessary, but to cut down on management and overhead costs, property was often turned over whenever possible to responsible federal and state agencies for protection. Further, TNC would decentralize, establishing state field offices that could keep closer watch on the land. Coinciding with its new focus, the national staff grew out of its basement quarters in Washington and moved just across the Potomac River into a high rise office building in Rosslyn, Virginia.

Emerging as well in the months and years that followed were the practical arguments for maintaining biotic diversity. Today any Conservancy staff member can cite a litany of benefits derived from little-known plants and animals—in medicine, engineering, and crop improvement. The Conservancy's new mission thrust practicality into an environmental arena that previously had been characterized by appeals to the public's sense of morality and love of beauty. Although morals and aesthetics still apply, the emphasis turned to "save this plant because we may need it someday" instead of "save this plant because we have no right to kill it."

The "practical" arguments are hard to dispute. The foods that sustain us come from a pitifully few plants, with many more awaiting discovery and use. What will be on the menu when disease or climate change wipe out the twenty or so plant species that now feed most of the world? The wild cousins of these plants often have resistances that can be hybridized into domestic strains. Little more than twenty years ago blight wiped out a fifth of the U.S. corn crop. By crossing field corn with a wild cousin, scientists altered the genetic makeup to resist the disease. Looking farther, the desirable qualities of non-relatives—even non-plants—may be recruited. The insect-repelling odor in a millipede found in North American forests might be transferable to cereal crops through genetic engineering.

A quarter of all prescription drugs used in the United States include plant extracts. Include across-the-counter pharmaceuticals and our medical dependency on natural ingredients is startling. The complex molecules in hundreds of plants and animals are beneficial to the human body in many ways, and often cannot be created artificially. On a simple level, many cooks keep a potted aloe

plant in their kitchens so its syrupy juice can soothe the pain of burns. Aspirin, perhaps the most common medicine known to modern man, derives from a willow. American Indians combined extracts from two types of cone flowers, a type of cedar, and a plant called false wild indigo as a disease preventative. Although the potion has since disappeared from American pharmacopoeia, tests conducted by a German firm among the elderly in a nursing home have indicated that the remedy, indeed, boosts the immune system.

Not surprisingly, many natural ingredients that are beneficial to human health are strangely compatible with the human body. Oil from cashew nuts has been found to fight tooth decay and other bacterial infections. Bamboo extracts have shown the ability to inhibit bacterial growth. More research into these properties may give the food industry a natural preservative more acceptable to consumers than chemicals whose effects on our bodies are uncertain.

A half century ago soldiers in Yunan province in China carried into battle certain plant extracts that brought almost miraculous mending when applied to a fresh wound. The recipe for the medicine, handed down from son to son by the local warlord, was lost when one patriarch produced no male lineage and refused to impart the knowledge to his daughters. Modern Chinese pharmacologists have identified the key ingredient in a trillium plant that is environmentally threatened. They are now producing the plant domestically while they search for the entire formula. In the west, it has been observed in hospitals that surgical thread made of material from the shells of certain insects and crustaceans dissolves in a sewed-up wound and promotes its healing.

Bee venom is used in the treatment of arthritis. Foxglove is a lovely garden flower but also the source of digitalis, a stimulant for a failing heart. With all these examples, it seems possible to imagine that if all life on earth, with all its variations, sprang from simple organic molecules and amino acids, perhaps all

ingredients once existed somewhere for near-perfect wholeness.

The search for these remaining keys to our survival and comfort has barely begun. Of all the plants and animals we know on this earth, only one in a hundred has been tested for possible benefit. And the species we have not even identified yet far outnumber those that we have. We destroy them before we discover them and determine how they might be useful.

The web that holds all life together is still under appreciated and little understood. Homeowners may wonder what possible good could come to them from the existence of mice. And yet, in the largest sense, the mouse is the staff of life for innumerable small carnivores. Without mice they might turn to other small mammals and that in turn devour insects. Without avian enemies the insects could flourish, threatening our food crops. In desperation we would apply more chemicals, perhaps finally tipping the toxic scale against our own existence. Thus, for want of a mouse, a world could be lost.

The now-extinct dodo bird once fed on the fruit of the tree *Calvaria major.* After the last dodo died in 1680 no new "dodo trees" sprouted. Nearly three hundred years later when all but thirteen of the ancient trees had disappeared, a scientist discovered that the grinding process in the dodo's craw had caused the seeds to germinate. The trees are now being reproduced by artificially abrading the seeds, a close call for *Calvaria.* What else depended on the dodo tree? What about the dodo itself? Did we lose a great source of food in those large, fruit-eating, slow-moving, flightless birds? What suffered or proliferated with the disappearance of the great auk, a large, diving sea bird once common on America's Atlantic coast?

Does the cure for cancer lie in the grizzly bear? Probably not. Some species may have no monetary worth but are fascinating to behold. If a grizzly has no value why do we thrill to the sight of it in the wild or stare at it in a zoo? Might its fearsome power remind us of our own limitations, our mortality? Children seem to need monsters. Perhaps adults need them as well, to excite their imaginations, to keep them humble.

Despite the numerous hints we have of the importance of every living species, we are wiping them out at the rate of at least three a day. Our increasingly urban population falls more and more out of touch with the natural world beyond the pavement. It follows that urbanites attach less and less importance to holding on to an insect or plant they have never heard of, let alone seen. "Ask the average person how they feel about the environment and they think clean air, clean water," said Nat Williams, director of government relations at TNC national headquarters. And, as Bob Jenkins observed, "There might be some feeling for nice landscapes, but little emotional involvement for the bugs and plants that make it work."

Our sensitivities are improving but still have far to go. Surveys have shown

OPPOSITE:
An aerial view shows remnant snow in summer on a high ridge in the Marshall Wilderness area on the Eastern Front of the Rocky Mountains.

RIGHT:
Bunchberries brighten a forest floor in autumn.

that the American people, given a choice of damming a stream for recreation or preserving an endangered species that lives there, will oppose the dam. But if the dam is to provide hydroelectric energy, they overwhelmingly favor it over the species. We have so crowded this planet with our own kind that our comfort and survival have become paramount in importance.

Stephen Kellert, a social ecologist at Yale University, studies public perceptions of wildlife in this country. He detects a strong interest in preserving species when conflicts with our own economic development arise, and believes that interest could be even stronger if the value of wildlife were better articulated. He lists seven values people attach to wildlife—some familiar, some not.

1. Recreational—the enjoyment gained by observing wildlife during an outdoor activity such as hiking or canoeing.

2. Ecological—the interrelation of flora and fauna to each other, and to the continuity of life, as well as to the maintenance of soils and other biogeochemical processes.

3. Moral—the belief that all species have a right to exist, and that we as humans have a duty to protect them.

4. Scientific—all species have the capability of advancing human knowledge and understanding of the natural world.

5. Aesthetic—many plants and animals are physically attractive.

6. Utilitarian—natural organisms are potential sources of benefit to human society in medicine, agriculture, and industry.

7. Cultural, symbolic, or historic—animals and plants function as expressions of group identity or may be the objects of special attachments. We relate strength to an elephant, intelligence to a fox, and have made the bald eagle our national symbol.

The relevance and range of these values is rarely pointed out to the public, Kellert says, when a conflict arises over existence of an endangered species and economic development. And preventing extinctions requires knowing what is about to become extinct. After proposing the rescue mission for The Nature Conservancy, Jenkins devised a system for making an inventory of what we have. It was an intricate method of surveying this country and then others, area by area, and classifying plants and animals according to the degree of their peril.

The system was first established by TNC in cooperation with the government of South Carolina in 1974. It was called the State Natural Heritage Program, since it preserved the heritage left to the people there. Heritage Programs now exist in all fifty states. The Conservancy partially funds them in the beginning and the state in most cases eventually takes over the expenses and salaries of the surveyors.

Obviously neither people nor resources are available to survey every inch of ground. The two or three biologists assigned to each state rely heavily on the work of previous naturalists. One such source is the Conservancy's own parent organization, the Ecological Society, which had identified hundreds of natural areas important to plant and animal diversity in a book called *A Naturalist's Guide to the Americas*. Other sources included natural history museums which have been collecting specimens for more than a century. Another great debt is owed to "gentlemen biologists" of the turn of the century, when it was fashionable for the wealthy to muck about in the woods with butterfly net and magnifying glass in their spare time, collecting, identifying, and cataloguing species.

Scanning earlier records, today's TNC biologists determine which species are most in danger of disappearing in a given area and compare that population with the rest across the face of the earth. Species of concern are given a ranking

by a key of three letters and numbers one through five. If a plant is fairly well distributed in other parts of the world but rare in, say, the state of New Jersey, it is given a ranking of G3S1 (G-Global, S-State). The rarest species would, thus, be ranked G1S1, or rare worldwide and also rare in the state where they are found.

A biologist with the Maryland Natural Heritage Program, Daniel Boone is lanky, sandy-haired, and unsure of his descendancy from the historical figure of the same name. He shares, however, his predecessor's love of the outdoors. Whereas the famous frontiersman felt cramped by civilization, today's Dan Boone worries about civilization cramping the wildlife that remains. As he tramps a rocky outcrop on a bank of the Potomac River near Washington, D.C. he describes what he calls a micro-habitat: "When the river floods, this outcrop becomes an island. The floodwaters stir things up, uncovering seeds that have lain dormant for hundreds of years, digging up old pages from the past. And because it's sometimes an island some specialized plants and insects that you don't find anywhere else in this area stay isolated on these rocks."

To Dan the plants tell a story of the planet's history. "Here's whorled milkweed, a Midwestern plant rarely found on the East Coast," he says. "It's a survivor of an earlier time when this area had a different climate." In a crevice of rock he spies prickly pear cactus, today associated with the desert southwest. "I wish I could roll back the clock to the time when this area must have been covered with these," he says with excitement. "Plants can tell us a lot about the processes Earth has gone through."

In a small sandy area he finds a species whose well-being he has come to check. Yellow nailwort, a spike-leafed plant with a yellow blossom, is ranked by the Conservancy as a G2S1, meaning it is very rare globally and extremely rare in this state. "Don't know if there's any use for it yet, but there aren't many left," he says. "This little community looks healthy enough, but any kind of construction or change here could wipe it out."

By surveying plants and animals, buying the habitat when necessary, or merely advising those who own it, The Nature Conservancy has preserved thousands of endangered plants and animals on this planet. The "ark" of saved species, as the Conservancy likes to call its successes, is steadily enlarging, as is the public support that keeps it afloat. Memberships climbed to 300,000 by 1985, then doubled in the next five years. State chapters were added one by one until by 1990 the fiftieth was in place. In the United States alone the pockets of protected land now total more than 5.5 million acres. An international program has helped like-minded partner organizations protect 22 million acres. In this country, new additions continue at a rate that averages a thousand acres a day.

Islands of Life

To a high-flying Canada goose, the northeast coast of North America appears to be crumbling like a large cookie, with the fragments drifting out to sea. Some 3,000 islands dot the coast of Maine and like children to cookies, residents of an increasingly crowded continent are drawn to these bastions of privacy.

"Back in the 1950s you could buy an island for $350," said Mason Morfit, director of the Maine office of The Nature Conservancy. "Now anything that stays above water at high tide starts at $100,000."

Maine's Great Duck Island, only an hour's motor launch ride from the mainland, was bought in the early 1960s by a psychiatrist who was prompted by the lure of isolation from a troubled world to turn it into an open air clinic. The island's rocky beach fringes some 200 yards of gentle slope before dissolving into quiet stands of spruce. With or without professional help the 250-acre island seemed to offer a measure of therapy. The Conservancy bought the property for $325,000 in 1984 after the psychiatrist needed money for a divorce settlement and to defend a malpractice suit. The Conservancy dismantled the rustic yurts, geodesic domes, and log cabins that had been built among the trees, saving only one lodge on a grassy knoll for overnight visits by TNC preserve managers.

The island's residents of most concern to the Conservancy were Leach's storm

petrels, one of the most unusual birds in ornithology, and one whose numbers are diminishing. The name "petrel" derives from the old English word for Peter, as in St. Peter, who by Biblical accounts tried to walk on water like Jesus. The petrels also seem to attempt waterwalking, as they hover just above the ocean and patter the surface tentatively with their webbed feet while feeding on zooplankton called copepods. First observers saw them along the shoreline in great abundance after storms at sea, which they believed drove them inland. Hence the name storm petrel.

The largest breeding population in the U.S., perhaps 10,000 birds, nests among the spruce of Great Duck Island. Not in the trees but under them, in burrows dug in the soft earth of the needle-strewn forest floor. At the back of each burrow a single egg is laid and a chick eventually hatched. The sea-going parents call on their offspring only at night, the better to escape herring gulls that cruise just offshore and may snatch the robin-sized petrels from the air and make a meal of them. If it escapes the gauntlet of gulls, an adult petrel enters the burrow and regurgitates into its chick a provender of copepods, which have been pre-digested into a viscous oil.

The chicks wax fat on the caloric oil, but when they begin fledging the parents cease their visits. After a couple of restless weeks the hungry young birds waddle out of the burrows and eventually fly off to sea. When they mature and mate they often seek other islands to build their own nests, perhaps a case of petrel pique over their abandonment as juveniles.

One of hundreds of coastal properties acquired by The Nature Conservancy, Great Duck Island neatly encapsules the problems at our shores: crowded people in a complex world seek solace by the sea, and in doing so threaten life long adapted to land's end. Do we hearken to an evolutionary marine past in our relentless pilgrimage to saltwater? Or do we simply yearn for an uncluttered view and the seemingly endless possibilities offered by the ocean expanse?

As the real estate boom in Maine has shown, whatever draws us to the coast draws us to the offshore islands as well. Natural fortresses with miles-wide moats, they often retain fragments of an earlier America. That kind of fragment exists a continent away from Maine on California's Santa Cruz Island. Operated as a ranch by one family for half a century, this largest of the state's eight Channel Islands seems, at first glance, visually frozen in time.

When computers first began clicking in Santa Barbara across twenty-four miles of seawater, free-ranging cattle on Santa Cruz's 62,000 acres were still being rounded up by cowboys on horseback. The few roads on the island are still mere tracks that dip into rocky streams and wind around steep-sided hills, plied occasionally by four-wheel-drive vehicles. One can imagine a chunk of America breaking off from the mainland a century ago and floating out to sea.

Physically, of course, the land mass became separated millions of years ago and as a result became a haven for unique plants and animals. Of more than 600

LEFT, BELOW:
A seashell midden on Santa Cruz attests to earlier use of the island by Indians before whites arrived. Large, single-ranch operations probably minimized damage to the island that might have come with multiple ownership and diverse use.

OVERLEAF:
A miniature "lost world," Santa Cruz Island in California's Santa Barbara channel has two mountain ranges, a variety of eco-zones, and several subspecies of flora and fauna found nowhere else. To preserve their special qualities the Conservancy bought ninety percent of the 62,000-acre island, scene of a nineteenth-century-style ranching operation for decades. An early but sensitive priority was to eradicate feral sheep and pigs that denuded hilltops, promoted erosion, and threatened the existence of Santa Cruz's unique residents.

Cloistered beauty, giant coreopsis established its own beachhead for survival on Santa Cruz. Unlike this large dense flower, other species responded to the limited land mass by becoming smaller than normal.

species of marooned plants, 43 are restricted to the Channel Islands and eight are found only on Santa Cruz. Birds obviously find it easier to mingle with relatives on the mainland, but one of more than 261 species identified on the island is the Santa Cruz Island scrub jay, which is larger and darker than scrub jays found elsewhere. Among the thirteen naturally occurring mammals, the Santa Cruz fox seems to have forgotten fox ways. Smaller in stature than mainland foxes and fairly docile around people, it forages boldly by day instead of furtively at night. Like the fox, the Columbian mammoth that once lived here belies its name. Remains of the mammoth found on Santa Cruz reveal instead a tusked miniature; adults that stood only six feet high at the shoulders, probably because of environmental constraints in their limited world.

With its pristine shores, irregular shape, and no readily visible sign of habitation, the island itself appears like a virgin continent in miniature. Two mountain ranges wring rain from onshore clouds to create freshwater streams, creeks and springs, and biotic communities include forests, grasslands, beaches and dunes. Never developed as real estate, the island has been only significantly altered since the mid-nineteenth century by domestic livestock.

Cattle ranching helped preserve Santa Cruz but tarnished it as well. Over decades, sheep and hogs also raised there slipped through the net of periodic roundups and reverted to the wild, proliferating into thousands. The sheep, lean and elusive, nibbled high-altitude vegetation down to dust. Stiff-bristled razorbacks plowed the ground with their long, tusked snouts. A verdant isle began to bald at its crown and the only logical prospect for the future would have been that its unique environments for plants and animals dissolved into desert.

In 1978 Dr. Carey Staunton, whose family had operated the ranch since the 1930s, discussed his concerns about preservation of Santa Cruz with The Nature Conservancy. For $2.6 million the Conservancy bought a large interest in the island and undertook conservation management of the land.

Eliminating the destructive feral animals was the first order of business,

Conservancy researchers restrain a young feral pig in a study of damage inflicted by escaped porkers. Tusks protruding from this one's bloodied snout grow long and curved on older boars, sought as trophies by hunters of a bow and arrow club. TNC honored the club's lease, arranged with the ranch's previous owner, until the lease expired.

Balding hilltops show damage from feral sheep that escaped from ranch operations through the years. Reverting to wild ways they took to the high ground and warily eluded costly efforts to transplant them elsewhere. Volunteer TNC marksmen following humane guidelines eradicated the last of thousands in the late 1980s. More easily captured cattle, seen grazing on a distant slope and (above) being rounded up, were removed later.

with the 30,000 sheep a priority. Rounding them up alive, which was attempted by previous owners, proved too slow and costly. With the sheep denuding the island, shooting them with high-powered rifles by hand-picked hunting teams became the only viable alternative. To blunt protests by animal rights groups, ground rules for the hunters were set—clean kills when possible and quick euthanasia of the wounded.

"I wasn't sure how I'd deal with the killing part," said schoolteacher Sue Maurer, a mountaineer by hobby who had never hunted before. "None of us enjoy it, but we hated seeing the island destroyed as well. I did it because I believed in the program, and with the sheep removed the recovery of the island has been dramatic."

Shortly after Dr. Staunton died in 1987 the last of the sheep were eradicated and brown hilltops quickly turned green again. By the original purchase agreement, TNC inherited nine-tenths of the island. Cattle were removed and eradication of the pigs will begin when a hunting lease expires. Santa Cruz will be allowed to step even further back in time, reverting to habitat that existed before first European contact.

At 62,000 acres, Santa Cruz stood for years as the largest single TNC preserve. Still considered a jewel among TNC purchases, it was dwarfed in 1990 by the acquisition of several ecosystems in the 500-square-mile Gray Ranch in southwestern New Mexico. The 321,703-acre property encompasses ninety-five percent of the Animas Mountain range, and harbors a greater diversity of mammalian wildlife than many existing national park or wildlife refuges in the continental United States.

Once the property of George Hearst, father of publisher William Randolph Hearst, the property was offered for sale by more recent owners, the Gray Land and Cattle Company, in 1989. Fearing it would be developed in ways unfriendly

TOP:
Squeezed into a final corner, a rare species of succulent called *Dudleya nesiotica* exists only on Santa Cruz Island, and only on one point of the island.

ABOVE:
Just wingbeats away from others of its kind, the Santa Cruz Island scrub jay grew larger and darker than jays on the California mainland after centuries of separation. Of 261 other birds identified on the island, many commute occasionally across the fifteen miles of Santa Barbara Channel.

OPPOSITE:
Lupine injects a dash of encouraging color to the island that elsewhere is ribbed and brown from erosion. Vegetation quickly began recovering on Santa Cruz after elimination of unwanted animals.

to the ecology, the Conservancy bought the entire parcel, believed to be the largest private land acquisition in conservation history, for approximately $18 million. Careful management will bring protection to nearly 100 plant and animal species considered endangered, threatened, rare, or sensitive to human activities. Animals include mountain lions, the Animas ridge-nosed rattlesnake, the white-sided jackrabbit, two varieties of bats, Swainson's hawks, and golden eagles. Of some 718 species of plants more than 70 are rare or endangered, such as the night-blooming cereus, Wright's fish-hook cactus, and the white butterfly cactus. Scattered over the vastness are also thirteen significant sites of pre-Columbian Indian ruins dating from 1150–1400 A.D. A full inventory of this remote pocket of North America will take years.

Although it was operated as a cattle ranch for most of this century, the sheer size of the property protected most of it from human intrusion. Located in the far southwestern corner of New Mexico, isolated from any major cities

Cleaning occupies a mountain lion on a snowy Utah butte. Still hunted in western states as a threat to livestock, hard-pressed cougars find protection on large Conservancy purchases such as 500-square-mile Gray Ranch in New Mexico and the Rosillos Mountains in southwest Texas, now a national wildlife refuge.

by at least 200 miles, with no motels within 70 miles, it has escaped transgressions of even the very curious and adventurous. Most of it, encompassing both southwestern scrub desert and woodlands of the Sierra Madre, is virtually untrammeled wilderness, although cattle have grazed it since the early 1900s and will continue to do so for the time being.

"The success of operating Gray Ranch as a natural ecosystem depends to some extent on achieving the cooperation of the local people," said a TNC officer in national headquarters. "If they don't understand and respect what we're doing, they might not respect our attempts to keep the area natural. The entire culture in this area is built around cattle and ranching. We can't just walk in and change things overnight by eliminating cattle altogether."

M O S T P E O P L E associate the wild kingdom with the sweeping grandeur of Gray Ranch's open prairie or the mystery of unbroken forests, but the richest ecosystem in North America is found in the salt marshes along our coasts. A study of finfish and shellfish taken from salt marshes has shown yields valued at $80,000–$110,000 per acre, far more lucrative than a Kansas wheatfield, biologically richer in terms of productivity than a virgin woodland. And yet, oceanfront residential construction and farming have been emptying this coastal cornucopia for decades, by dredging and filling and by chemical pollution from agricultural runoff. Even with wetland preservation a frequent topic of newspaper headlines and stated government policy, we still lose some 18,000 acres of estuarine marshes each year.

In 1987 a large land purchase in Florida stopped fragmentation of salt marshes in one long stretch by stitching together 200 miles of nearly uninterrupted coastline. Portions of the "Big Bend"—where the state's northwest coast arcs toward Mississippi and Louisiana—had come under state and federal

O V E R L E A F :
A mosaic of salt marsh stretches away from the west coast of Florida, providing a valuable nursery for oceangoing fish later harvested as seafood. Shellfish and numerous birds also thrive in these tidal swamps, often decimated by dredge and fill operations to create seaside condominiums and houses. Working with state and federal agencies, The Nature Conservancy helped preserve a 200-mile long chain of protected lands where the peninsula arcs toward Louisiana, in what is known as Florida's Big Bend.

protection, with The Nature Conservancy aiding in the acquisitions at least half the time. At the top of the arc are St. Mark's National Wildlife Refuge and the Apalachicola Bay National Estuarine Sanctuary. Protected areas to the south include Gulf Hammock State Preserve, Lower Suwannee River National Wildlife Refuge, Crystal River State Preserve, and the Chassahowitzka National Wildlife Refuge. The largest gap in this string of wildness was closed in 1987 with the bargain purchase of 64,631 acres from the Procter and Gamble Corporation. At this writing the Big Bend acquisition represents one of TNC's biggest land deals east of the Mississippi.

A marsh is only as good as the land behind it. High ground of the Big Bend purchase extends five to ten miles inland, habitat for deer, black bear, bobcat, raccoon, and smaller mammals. The U.S. Fish and Wildlife Service may reintroduce the endangered Florida panther here when a captive breeding program develops more candidates. As a buffer against pollution runoff from further inland, TNC is buying more land along the Suwannee, Santa Fe, and Wacissa rivers that feed into Big Bend.

Visitors to this healthy marsh find that it floods the senses with its richness. Virtually inaccessible by land, it is best travelled by boat through the open channels formed by tidal movement. The lush cordgrass set to gentle swaying by the boat's bow wave and the gray muck beneath fill the nostrils with pungent smells. Feeding on detritus that settles to the bottom are mollusks, marine worms, insects, and crustaceans, themselves food for fish and birds. Wood storks and great blue herons stalk about in the company of other feathered foragers—great egrets, smaller herons, belted kingfishers, and terns.

Black mullet, red drum, spotted sea trout, and sheepshead grow to size here before moving to the open sea. Birds are the most visible. The marsh is breeding habitat for the seaside sparrow, clapper rail, marsh wren, and purple

ABOVE:
Lance-leafed trillium grow along the Apalachicola River in Florida. By The Nature Conservancy's system of ranking species according to their rarity, the plant's G3 rating means that globally it grows in a restricted range, and is thus imperiled.

RIGHT:
Quiet waters of the Apalachicola should stay peaceful thanks to Conservancy efforts. Since coastal marshes are only as healthy as the streams that feed them, the organization teamed with public agencies in protecting more than 170,000 acres fringing Florida waterways like this one.

gallinule to name a few; and it offers refuge in winter for the snowy plover and numerous waterfowl.

Shortly after its purchase by the Conservancy, the Big Bend property was resold to Florida, thanks to the "Save Our Coasts" program funded by the state's landmark real estate transfer tax that has since been copied elsewhere.

To control residential development in one of the fastest growing states, Florida has enacted legislation that requires each county to devise a land use plan. The legislation enraged land developers, especially in the Florida Keys, the strand of tiny islands trailing off the bottom of the continent like a ragged tail. Few Americans realize that some residents of the Keys attempted a halfhearted secession from the United States the same year, calling themselves the "Conch Republic" after the edible, trumpet-shaped mollusk, and creating their own passport and flag. Ignored by the federal government, the rebellion fizzled into an amusing footnote.

Popular with tourists since Route 1 long ago laced the limestone islands together, the Keys exploded with development after the multimillion-dollar upgrading of a freshwater pipeline in the early 1980s. Houses invaded many of the islands' forested high grounds known as hardwood hammocks, subtropical ecosystems with unique adaptations to isolation in the Keys. Aside from the importance of preserving their unique qualities, problems with sewage treatment and disposal make it clear that the Keys have built-in limits to growth.

Owners of real estate in the Keys may be the most ardent anti-environmentalists left in the nation. "The Land Use Act was shoved down our throats by a government that cares more about animals than it does about people," railed a realtor on Big Pine Key. "They want to keep the human population down in the Keys and they're doing it by telling us where we can and we can't build houses on our own property."

One lifetime resident of the Keys held onto a large piece of open hammock for decades, planning a comfortable retirement by selling eventually to a developer. Retirement and new restrictions came at roughly the same time. Suddenly houses couldn't be built within fifty feet of the water, and a state permit is now required before mangrove can even be cut for access roads.

The Nature Conservancy, competing with developers for the purchase of properties, sees a complex and fragile ecosystem under siege. Here the zones of temperate North America and subtropical Florida meet the tropics of the Caribbean, resulting in rare communities clinging to life on these limestone islands. What special qualities, TNC questions, has the struggle for survival given these species that might be of use to us?

The list of imperiled species in the Keys is long for such a small and scattered ecosystem. Best known is a deer no taller than a great dane, for which land was first set aside in the 1950s. But construction is shrinking the habitat of the toy-like, white-tailed Key deer despite establishment of National Key Deer Refuge in 1954. Increased road traffic kills nearly fifty a year, out of a total population of some 250. Over the past five years, with help from the Conservancy, the Wilderness Society and other environmental groups, refuge land owned and managed by the U.S. Fish and Wildlife Service has increased by 1,000 acres to a total of nearly 8,000.

Elsewhere, 4,000 acres have been preserved for some of the last American crocodiles, and negotiations are underway for protection of Schaus's swallowtail butterfly, the Key tree cactus, and the Key Largo wood rat. While efforts for the soft-eyed deer seem above reproach, those for some of the other endangered species rankle land-hungry speculators. "They spend millions to keep a rat alive while Miami spends millions to kill rats," said the realtor on Big Pine Key. "They say this wood rat is special, but a rat is a rat. And they spend

ABOVE:
Making its mark for posterity, an apple snail leaves a trail of eggs on the underside of a leaf at Wakulla Springs. Saving the springs, part of the Big Bend program, secured a habitat not only for the snail but also for its main predator, the limpkin.

OPPOSITE, ABOVE:
Moorhen mother and chicks patter over shoreline water plants on the Wakulla.

OPPOSITE, BELOW:
A threatened limpkin strolls over aquatic plants while devouring another threatened creature, the apple snail, mainstay of its diet. Partial to fresh, unpolluted streams, the snail thrives in the protected Wakulla and, therefore, so does the limpkin.

71

millions to preserve the crocodile, one of the nastiest creatures on earth. It makes no sense."

To others it makes such perfect sense that an air of urgency pervades those trying to rescue the Keys from further development. "When you consider the natural biological diversity of species here and the special adaptations they've made," said Charles Olson of the Florida Key Land Trust, which works with TNC to save land, "I can think of few areas where preservation is more critical."

NO HIVE OF land barons, The Nature Conservancy will turn over properties to third parties it feels will manage them in a way that protects endangered species. Sometimes they simply make possible a real estate sale to the federal government by acting as a silent partner between buyer and seller, or donor and recipient. In 1984 TNC arranged a gift to the federal government of 118,000 acres of a peninsula on the North Carolina coast owned by the Prudential Insurance Company. U.S. Fish and Wildlife called it the Alligator River National Wildlife Refuge and released into it the first red wolves ever reintroduced to the wild from captivity.

When European colonists first settled in America the red wolf ranged over the entire east coast. Smaller than the better-known gray, or timber wolf, it had been completely eliminated from the wild, surviving only by captive breeding. The peninsula in North Carolina offered an attractive testing site for wolf reintroduction, since it is bounded on one side by the two-mile-wide Alligator River and on two other sides by the Albemarle and Croatan Sounds.

The red wolves' new home was wild and wooded but often damp and spongy, a land form known as pocosin. Over centuries the poorly drained soils turn peaty with a carpet of sphagnum moss building up over them. Trees and

brush grow above the carpet leaving a landscape too soft for farming and too densely vegetated for grazing or even for hunting—a haven for wildlife. Rabbits, opossums, raccoons, muskrats, nutria, small rodents, and an occasional deer would provide food for the red wolves. Black bear would be their only natural enemy.

In the fall of 1986 the Fish and Wildlife Service transferred five pairs of captive-raised red wolves to the refuge negotiated by TNC. A public relations campaign preceded the animals for the benefit of the thousand or so people living on the peninsula, most of them engaged in fishing and services. In public meetings biologists patiently explained to folks already concerned with keeping the economic wolf from the door that the real thing posed no threat to them or their children.

So shy and unaggressive are red wolves that the use of tranquilizers is not necessary in handling them. "If you can corner them in a pen they often just lie flat and let you pin them down," said John Taylor, director of the refuge. "They just give up when you grab them by the scruff of the neck. You couldn't do that with a gray wolf."

Wolves raised on dog food had to be taught how to forage for themselves. The animals were kept in 50-by-50-foot holding pens in the forest for six months, each pair in a separate location. A full-time caretaker monitored each pen, taking pains to avoid being seen by the animals, tossing road-killed small animals over the one boarded side of the wire cages. Gradually, live-trapped prey was introduced into the cages for rehearsals in the art of chase and kill.

In early summer of 1987 handlers wired open the doors to the pens and the wolves were allowed to leave on their own. They wore radio collars to track their whereabouts. As expected, a life of freedom was no piece of cake. In the first two and a half years, four wolves died while crossing highways at night.

OPPOSITE, ABOVE: Freedom didn't come easily for red wolves raised in captivity. At a halfway house pen at its release site, a wolf is placed in a basket for weighing to see how it is adjusting to a new diet of wild rodents and raccoons.

OPPOSITE, BELOW: The burnished coat that gives the red wolf its name gleams in the sun. During the wolves' six-month period of adjustment inside pens, caretakers tried to stay out of sight so the animals would not become acclimated to humans. This photograph was taken from a viewing hole in a plywood barrier. After six months the doors to the pens were wired open so the wolves could leave on their own.

Two succumbed to disease. A fight between two females damaged one so severely that it was put out of its misery. One large, strong male that had adapted well to the hunt choked to death on the kidney of a raccoon. The faithfully beeping radio collar of another wolf was traced to inside the belly of an alligator.

A mortality of nearly forty per cent struck the first released wolves, and the original ten had to be augmented by the release of more captive-bred animals. In the several litters born in the wild, hookworm killed most of the pups, although survivors fare better than their parents. "We've noticed that wild-born wolves don't frequent highways as much as the captive animals did," said Taylor.

To increase the survival rate of newly wild wolves the U.S. Fish and Wildlife Service began releasing adult pairs on roadless East Coast islands, then transporting them to Alligator River after their litters grew strong. Coupled with the captive release program and the slow but steady buildup of savvy wild-born pups, the program is deemed a success.

Success received a boost in 1990 when the wolf range was nearly doubled with the purchase of 104,000 acres of woodland west of Alligator River Refuge by the Richard King Mellon Foundation, which then donated the land for use as a wildlife refuge. The additional land adjoined the Alligator River and greatly enlarged the area where the transplanted wolves could roam.

To maintain genetic diversity the red wolf recovery team hopes to build a wild population of 200 backed up by some 300 wolves maintained in captivity. Modest though its numbers may be now, a wild native has returned to eastern forests. The wolf project offers hope to other species now clinging to survival in cages or isolated wild pockets, such as the black-footed ferret and the Florida panther.

The U.S. Fish and Wildlife Service functions as a preserver of certain species. With other agencies, TNC has found that a partnership sometimes works better in correcting the mistakes incurred by human use. The Bureau of Land Management oversees the biggest spread of real estate in the United States, allowing activities such as mining, logging, and grazing on public land. Sometimes those activities, along with much more intense activity on nearby private lands, force already hard-pressed species into precarious corners.

The San Joaquin Valley kit fox found at least a safe corner when the Conservancy undertook a cooperative agreement with BLM for protection of Carrizo Plain, a chunk of California's Central Valley. A distinct subspecies, the kit fox survives in natural grasslands and scrub brush, left in short supply by human pressures. Of some two million acres of natural savannah that once covered California lowlands, less than one percent now remains. The fox, along with the blunt-nosed leopard lizard and the giant kangaroo rat, is now ranked on the federal list of endangered species.

A decade ago Carrizo Plain in the southwestern part of the Central Valley was drifting toward the fate of other California grasslands. Dryland farming in wheat and barley was altering the landscape and unregulated cattle grazing had stunted grass down to bare soil that blew and washed away. Tule elk—smaller than the Rocky Mountain version—and pronghorn antelope had been hunted out of existence. Before the California condor went into captivity it soared over Carrizo's 180,000 acres in search of food, along with twelve species of raptors. Carrizo Plain remains a prime candidate for reintroduction of condors to the wild.

About half the plain was owned privately and the other half was held by the Bureau of Land Management. In early 1988 The Nature Conservancy bought 82,000 acres and reached an agreement with BLM that it would manage the government's half as well. In TNC's management plan grazing by cattle could

Not crafty enough to escape the endangered species list, the San Joaquin kit fox nearly succumbed to a changing California landscape. Farming and overgrazing had decimated the home of this distinct subspecies, 180,000 acres of grasslands known as Carrizo Plain located 150 miles north of Los Angeles. In buying half the tract and working with the Bureau of Land Management to restore the remainder, the Conservancy is preserving the last significant stretch of savannah that once covered California's Central Valley. In the process it also guarantees a home for the fox and several other locally endangered and threatened species.

TOP:
A San Joaquin antelope squirrel strikes a prayerful pose, as if in thanks for return of food and cover in Carrizo Plain.

ABOVE:
A young opossum gamely negotiates a slender tree branch on Carrizo Plain.

RIGHT:
The Englemann Oak was a common species in the hills around Los Angeles before being replaced by subdivisions. The trees' twisted branches now find room to stretch on the Conservancy-owned Santa Rosa Plateau in California.

continue, but on a much smaller scale, to simulate the grazing done by wild ungulates before ranching began. Volunteers help plant shrubs of saltbush, Mormon tea, and winterfat to recreate the habitat that existed decades ago.

The corrective planting has been slowed by persistent drought in the area, but already increases can be seen in both brushy cover and perennial grasses. With their habitats thus enhanced, the fox, blunt-nosed lizard, and kangaroo rat appear out of immediate danger. Tule elk and pronghorn were shipped in from northern California and are proliferating. Carrizo Plain, a remnant of the original California valleys, is on the mend.

IN ADDITION to its partnerships with federal agencies, The Nature Conservancy sometimes works with small communities as well, usually without owning a local acre. On a bump of land just off Rhode Island, Keith Lewis watched the home of his youth and his ancestors disappearing under the onslaught of development. "We're within the reach of Boston and New York and the pressures are enormous," said the stocky merchant seaman with the Captain Ahab beard, a sixth generation resident of little Block Island. "About 700 people live here year-round, but in summer the population swells to 10–15,000."

Change began centuries ago when settlers from Massachusetts colony arrived on the three-by-seven mile island in 1661, probably because it offered grazing free of predators for their livestock. Original oaks, maples, and hickories were felled for buildings and firewood, and even the earliest photographs show a treeless landscape. The Lewis family bought an acreage in 1817 and grazing gave way to tillage of potatoes and feed grains for barter on the mainland. In the early 1900s the first hotels were built. Block Island has seen escalating tourism and summer home building since then.

OPPOSITE:
A grassland turned deathtrap when severe overgrazing stripped Carrizo Plain of vegetation. Successive years of drought nearly scored a knockout punch. In its management plan for the area TNC allows limited grazing by cattle while re-introducing natural herbivores such as Tule elk and pronghorn. Volunteers working on weekends have also planted shrubs and grasses common to the area.

Alarmed at shrinking open space, Keith Lewis joined the Block Island Conservancy formed by his father. He later helped to set up the Block Island Land Trust. Both groups were long on concern and short on expertise in saving land and enlisted help from The Nature Conservancy. TNC negotiators, with their knowledge of tax laws and possible benefits to sellers through charitable donations, helped Block Islanders purchase chunks of property—some harboring hard-pressed species—at bargain prices. Within five years protective ownership of open space by the environmental groups grew from four percent to seventeen percent. On other properties the Conservancy helped arrange conservation easements preventing activities that might endanger upland sandpipers, grasshopper sparrows, and barn owls that burrow in steep cliff faces.

Never wealthy, Lewis cut back on his voyages as an engine room chief on ocean-going vessels so he could devote more time to conservation: "I just work enough to make what I need." Property that could have made him a millionaire he sold to the Conservancy at a bargain rate that allowed him to pay off his mortgage, and he agreed to conservation easements on the remainder.

"At this stage in my life I just want to do conservation work," Lewis said. "It's my goal to show that conservation makes good economic sense. I tell people on Block Island that if we keep some of the land open it improves the quality of life and keeps property values up. And if it allows some scientific research on the land we've saved, it keeps a few people coming here for reasons other than summer vacations, which is good for the island economy.

"On a larger scale, anywhere along a coastline, it makes sense as well. Fish need clean water to live in, and it's cheaper to let nature purify runoff by leaving large natural areas than have us try to do it with technology.

"I think it's interesting to see if democracy can deal with environmental issues to everyone's satisfaction. After all, we are the smallest town in the smallest state. We are still governed by town meeting—the purest form of democracy. If we can handle these issues here I hold out some hope for humanity."

D E M O C R A C Y went to work in Wisconsin when the Conservancy helped draft laws and regulations that preserved the beauty of a quiet stream steeped in history, although no threatened species was targeted. The Brule River in northern Wisconsin had been a water highway for French voyageurs, a fifty-mile link between Lake Superior and the Mississippi drainage. It remained unusually pristine after becoming a retreat for the wealthy and influential, while clear cut logging was muddying streams elsewhere in the north woods. Calvin Coolidge had a summer playhouse beside the Brule. The Ordways, of Minnesota Mining and Manufacturing Company (3M), still own 3,600 acres along its banks.

Landowners along the Brule wanted forests, quiet, and trout fishing, not scalped watersheds. They built houses back from the stream and blended them into the surroundings, respected each other's privacy, and avoided commercial development. Old trees grew older and other species thrived in their natural undergrowth. In the early 1950s, however, four hundred acres came up for sale. Fearing a subdivision, the other property owners formed the Brule River Association and bought the tract. That land, and the private holdings each association member held along the river, they loosely referred to as "the preserve."

Their own dedication to the northern Shangri-la was obvious, but they were less sure about their heirs. Some who would eventually own a piece of the preserve lived far away and had never formed emotional ties with the beauty of the Brule. Nothing in the association's heart-felt bylaws could prevent a member from selling to a developer, whose volume construction might change the stream for everyone.

Someone in the association knew of The Nature Conservancy's ability to protect private property, and TNC was invited in to help. In numerous meetings with the landowners, Conservancy workers drew up conservation easements that froze development within the property held by all association members. The easements were tailored to each landowner's individual needs in case some additional inoffensive construction was anticipated—a guest cottage or another outbuilding.

The Brule's banks were protected, but then an unforeseen invasion began shattering the quiet ambience—modern voyageurs riding inflated inner tubes. For twenty of its fifty miles the river drops 300 feet, creating whitewater relished by trout and tubers alike. What started as a harmless activity by a few people turned into loud and frequent flotillas of boisterous, destructive fun-seekers. Tubers crawled out on the banks to leave defecation and litter. The splashing and yelling of beered-up groups made fishing impossible, according to one association member.

To protect the historic stream and its century-old biota, the Wisconsin legislature banned tubing on the Brule, believed to be the first such law in the nation. TNC assistance in writing the law and quietly urging its passage was done in its usual low-profile, no-headline manner.

"The Nature Conservancy?" responded a local fisherman wetting a line in the clear, trout thoroughfare downstream from the Association's lands. "Never heard of it."

IF TROUT STREAMS were human we'd say preventive medicine saved the Brule. Applying the same analogy, we find that a more famous waterway several states away was brought back from the dead. Two decades ago, ranching and farming had sullied a gem of the old West, a magical tributary named Silver Creek near Ketchum, Idaho.

In a reverse of the usual dynamics of waterways—small tributaries feeding larger arteries—Silver Creek is fed by the larger Wood River, about a mile away. Water from the Wood percolates underground down a long, gradual incline through glacial till before it comes up against a lava block and is forced to the surface. The numerous springs of crystal-clear water wander through a marsh before coming together in a single channel that is further fed by other freshets boiling to the surface along the way.

The clear water flowing over a gravelly bottom, slowed by freshwater vegetation called chara, creates ideal conditions for invertebrates that feed trout, and for the trout themselves, and for fishermen who seek the wily trout. Ernest Hemingway was drawn to Silver Creek nearly half a century ago, but through an odd twist of fate the author of the short story "Big Two-Hearted River" never fished this trout mecca. Eager to do so he had his fly-fishing gear shipped to Ketchum in a trunk, but it was lost in transit and never found.

"He was so depressed that he never replaced the gear," said his son Jack, an even more devoted fly fisherman who lives near Ketchum. "He hunted along it though. We used to canoe down the creek, one of us the paddler in back and the other the gunner in front, and around almost every bend we would raise ducks."

Had he lived until the mid-1970s the Nobel Prize-winning writer would not have recognized the once-lovely stream. The land in many places was tilled to within a foot of its banks, which were trampled into muck elsewhere by cattle. Drainage ditches had been cut to dry out the marshy headwaters to create even more grazing. Silver Creek was becoming muddy creek, so opaque that the bottom could no longer be seen, so silted that the bottom-growing vegetation and marine life was changing. No one was more disturbed than the son of Ernest Hemingway.

In 1976 Jack Hemingway learned that one of the major owners along Silver Creek might be interested in selling his portion. He contacted The Nature Conservancy, which acquired a number of properties totaling some 750 acres along the stream. Elsewhere TNC acquired conservation easements for careful management of land, bringing protection to nearly 2,000 acres bearing on some twelve miles of the waterway. A major facelifting began.

Cattle were barred from access to the creek, and vegetative buffers were required between croplands and the water. The ditches that drained the marsh were plugged and the water reverted to its original pattern of slow, clean seepage into the main channel. Volunteers built fences to keep out the cattle and waded in the muck to replace original vegetation that had been lost. Some of the plants that were returned to streambanks were noxious to agricultural practices, so a light periodic spraying program was undertaken at the edge of the property to prevent their spreading.

The stream responded. Clear water returned and trout thrived. Rushes and willows grew along its banks until now Silver Creek is once again an emerald and blue oasis, home to seventy-seven different species of birds in addition to the fish. Blue heron and sandhill cranes wade its shallows, and both red-winged and yellow-headed blackbirds serenade from the reeds. Of the 7,000–8,000 visitors that sign in annually at the little hut on a hill overlooking Silver Creek Preserve, one in seven is a birder.

The remainder come from around the world to test their skills against wily torpedoes in what has again become a world class trout stream. The fish feed in precise synchronization to the hatching and development of the stream's invertebrates, so fly selection depends on careful study of the water. The swirl of tails at the surface probably means insects such as mayflies are appearing on the bottom, so the fish have their heads down, waiting for a snack to emerge. Noses breaking the surface and leaving bubbles signal fish taking larvae that are floating while unfolding their wings.

The slow current causes little distortion on the surface, giving the fish time to study suspicious-looking bait. The big trout—five and six pounds—have learned wariness from experience, for fishing is allowed only on a "catch and release" program.

Once again marsh hawks wheel overhead and mallards lift off the water when walking fishermen round a bend. Ernest Hemingway once wrote of a war-damaged young man paying a therapeutic call on a trout-rich stream: "He was there, in the good place. He was in his home where he had made it." A lot of people who helped re-make a good place feel that way about Silver Creek.

EXEMPLARY though the reconstruction of Silver Creek might have been, it was a departure from the Conservancy's usual insistence on saving extremely rare species and community remnants. Other projects, while true to TNC philosophy, have also missed the profile.

On summer days in Bracken Cave near San Antonio, Texas, Mexican free-tailed bats hang from the ceiling in the world's largest known concentration of mammals by weight and by volume, some twenty million or more. By night they pour from the cave mouth in a stream so thick that it appears on the radar of San Antonio airport several miles away. While they are gone the young left behind cling to the cave ceiling. Amazingly, in the swirl of millions of satin wings and velvet bodies that marks the dawn's return, each adult finds its own bat pup by homing in on the distinctive squeak.

Plentiful though the bats might be there, Bracken Cave holds forty percent

of the known population of Mexican free-tailed bats, a species concentration that makes bat-lovers nervous. San Antonio development is stretching toward the cave entrance, which is owned by the Marbach family. Those who might consider it good riddance to lose twenty million macabre Halloween symbols should consider the following: if each of the insectivorous bats devours thirty mosquitoes each night (light fare) it amounts to the biologic removal of more than a half-billion itch-makers daily. In cooperation with Bat Conservation International, The Nature Conservancy has negotiated a voluntary agreement with the Marbachs that no activity will be undertaken around the cave that might adversely affect the bats within.

The rarities in another cave the Conservancy helped save appear to be geological rather than biologic. In 1974, two cavers discovered a previously unknown cavern in Arizona and kept its secret for fourteen years. Curiosity-seekers, they knew, could pilfer some of the outstanding features in the 2.5-mile-long cave, including some of the world's longest known "soda straws." The thin, hollow stalactites, often a mere quarter inch in diameter, are usually 12 to 24 inches long; one in this cave stretched 22 feet.

Four years after they made their discovery, cavers Randy Tufts and Gary Tenen revealed it to the Kartchner family, who owned the ranchland above the structure. The cave's secrets remained intact for seven more years, when state officials and The Nature Conservancy were enlisted to aid in its protection. Arizona wanted to create a state park, but feared that seeking appropriations would bring unwanted publicity. The Conservancy quietly took an option to buy the cave, and elaborate security measures including laser detectors were set up to guarantee that no unauthorized entrance would go unnoticed. After the state acquired financing the Conservancy signed over the option, and Kartchner Cave was expected to open as a state park in 1992 or 1993.

OPPOSITE:
A flood of Mexican free-tailed bats flows from Bracken Cave near San Antonio, Texas, heading for an evening feed that includes millions of mosquitoes. One of nature's most unloved and under-appreciated denizens, bats not only help control insects but also may hold some physical quality of benefit to mankind.

OVERLEAF:
Inside Arizona's Kartchner Cavern: Unusual formations include the largest known cave column and thin stalactites called "soda straws," one measuring twenty-two feet. To avoid destruction by careless explorers, discovery of the 2.5-mile-long cave was kept secret for fourteen years.

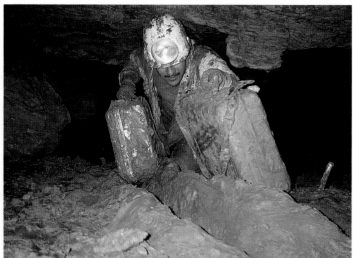

"We saved no living species that we know of," said an officer in the Arizona TNC chapter, "but we did set up a congenial relationship with the state that makes it easier to work on future projects."

FLYING OVER farming or residential areas, who hasn't seen reddish soil feeding into rivers from streams and fanning into bays from the rivers? Wounded land bleeds through arteries of water. Less visible until they alter vegetation or ignite algal bloom are the chemicals and nutrients that leach from agricultural fields. Sometimes riverine ecosystems change because the stream itself has been robbed of water for irrigation or urban use. The Colorado River, which once flowed without interruption to the Pacific, is now sipped dry somewhere in the desert Southwest.

In America's West, rights to water are as real as rights to land. A deed is given for water rights to a stretch of river, water commissioners monitor the rate of its flow, and individuals sometimes hire "ditch riders" to guard against stream burglary. Water, like land, has long been seen as a resource to be exploited. But the massive drawdown of streams has alarmed environmentalists, who argue that not only single species but whole ecosystems are threatened in the process.

Colorado set the precedent for the entire West in 1876 with a water doctrine that attempted to apportion streams equitably. Removal of water was regarded as its only legitimate function. Nearly a century later, in 1973, the same state approved an "in-stream flow law," which held that leaving water in a stream could be a beneficial use of it as well. Since western water rights are essentially property rights, the Conservancy began applying its usual techniques of buying, trading, and seeking donations of those rights so it could protect ecosystems that depended on stream flow.

OPPOSITE,
ABOVE LEFT:
A clutch of Mexican free-tailed bats hangs from the ceiling of Bracken Cave, a seasonal roost in the path of expanding San Antonio. The massing of twenty million bats in the cave is believed the largest single concentration of mammals in the world. Their guano buildup on the cave floor was once mined as fertilizer.

OPPOSITE,
ABOVE RIGHT:
Approaching one of Kartchner's large chambers, an Arizona parks employee lugs camera gear through a muddy crawlway.

OPPOSITE, BELOW:
An underground pool of mud doesn't stop explorers in Arizona's Kartchner Cave, a trove of several rare geologic structures. In an unusual project, the Conservancy quietly helped Arizona protect the cave from souvenir hunters until the state could buy it for a park. Although no known living species were saved, the cooperative effort may ease the way in future negotiations with Arizona.

In TNC's first major water project the Colorado office received a donation of 300 cubic feet per second (cfs), which in western water jargon refers to the amount of water that passes a given point in one second. The gift from Pittsburg and Midway Coal Mining Company, a subsidiary of Chevron, was valued at $7 million, and helps protect the spectacular scenery and important biological community of Black Canyon, through which the Colorado River runs.

Acquiring water rights so a stream can continue flowing is not as simple as it sounds. In Colorado, for example, only the state's water conservation board can own water rights for in-stream flow, so the Chevron gift of 300 cfs had to be turned over immediately to the board. A 1987 state law says, however, that the party turning over the instream flow rights retains some control over its use, to the point of suing the state board if it does not comply.

Arizona and some other states, on the other hand, allow a private entity to own in-stream flow rights, as demonstrated by The Nature Conservancy. In 1983 the organization acquired from the state board the right to a certain amount of water flowing through TNC's Ramsey Canyon Preserve. The Conservancy then left the water in the stream to protect the emerald ecosystem in an otherwise arid region, the first private holder of water rights in the West to do so.

IT IS NOT hard to believe that saving a rare species of plant or animal might hold some benefit for Homo sapiens. For many people, however, saving entire plant communities—especially ones that seem ordinary—because of the way in which they came together requires a stretch of the imagination. For subtleties in the preservation game, it is hard to beat Cross Ranch Preserve in North Dakota.

When Lewis and Clark journeyed up the Missouri River in 1806 their views of the rolling prairie and riverside woodlands were little different from what can be seen along the 5,000-acre preserve today. The only human dwellers in that era were Mandan Indians, whose lodges of mud and sticks have long since collapsed and left small raised outlines on the prairie floor. Pocket gophers still excavate shards of flint and pottery, kicking them out with the dirt around their mounds.

The river the explorers rode was different then, a wilder, meandering force, an architect that constantly carved banks on one side and built fertile new shores on the other. Because unpredictability was the enemy of settlement and "civilization," the Missouri since then has been collared by dams and reservoirs along most of its 360-mile length.

As it sweeps past Cross Ranch in a large and somewhat irregular arc, the river cuts into the outside bank and deposits the soil picked up there slightly downriver and on the opposite side. Over years, the river gradually moves in the direction of the cut bank, and the new terrain on the opposite shore builds up in a series of terraces. On those stairsteps—each thirty to forty years in the making—grows a distinct succession of flood-plain forest.

On the latest deposit of land next to the water's edge, little cottonwood sprouts shoot up in the direct sunlight and moist silt. At the next level, now further ashore, grow cottonwoods up to forty years old. The oldest trees, at the third level, are nearing the century mark, with thick trunks and large, spreading canopies. Unable to reproduce themselves at that stage because of the shade they cast and the deep leaf litter, they are gradually replaced by green ash, box elder, and American elm. As the loop becomes deeper the current now begins cutting into the near bank, cutting into the forest it had previously built up, and the process begins all over again.

Does a remedy for AIDS lie within that process of shifting soil and cycling

woodlands? The most optimistic Conservancy manager would hesitate to suggest that possibility. Instead, significance is seen in the natural dynamic that evolved over millions of years, one that shapes life and land in ways that we have not even attempted to understand. What aquatic and forest creatures came to depend on the food supplies generated by the river's work? Did the constant change affect plants in ways that might benefit mankind? How many dozens, hundreds, perhaps thousands of unseen organisms adjusted to special roles in that slow pageant at the river bend, and do those roles hold any secrets that we might find interesting?

Answers to these questions will never be found if all Missouri River banks are stabilized by cement revetments, or the forest cover is stripped for timber and the rich soil farmed in monoculture crops. The modern tendency is to wipe the slate clean before studying its contents. The purchase of Cross Ranch allows riverbank dynamics to continue, and for scientists to study them.

The view of the prairie further up the banks at Cross Ranch may appear similar to the one seen by Lewis and Clark from canoes, but up close, life is changing there as well. Bison were once the primary grazers, and have now joined cattle on the ranch. The two ungulates feed on different plants and in different places. With their shaggy shoulder coats buffalo prefer the breezy hilltops, while cattle bunch in the shade of the tree-lined ravines. The trampling and feeding of the cattle in the ravines alters the plant communities found there, which are much different from those on open prairie. Without proper management the woody draws gradually disappear, and the forbs that thrived in their shade disappear with them.

A grass-roots effort saved the grasses and woodlands of Cross Ranch. Its conservation-minded previous owners, Bob and Gladys Levis, wanted to sell the 5,000 acres to North Dakota, but a referendum on the acquisition, which

OPPOSITE:
Weeds to many a train passenger, this plant community on the Amtrack right-of-way in Michigan is a remnant of early prairie, never plowed or replaced. After identifying a number of threatened plants alongside the tracks, the Conservancy leased six strips in southwest Michigan from the National Rail Passenger Corporation (Amtrack) and now protects and manages the strips.

The horse-high grass of the Great Plains, big bluestem, has a triple-pronged head that earned it the nickname "turkeyfoot." Although nutritious for animals and resistant to drought, big bluestem has been replaced on the plains by cereal crops and more vulnerable orchard grasses preferred by domestic livestock. This bluestem patch endures at the Conservancy's Bakertown Fen in Michigan, sixty-two acres containing six plant species that are threatened in the state.

would have doubled the size of the state park system, was narrowly defeated in the 1980 election. The owners then approached the Conservancy, which launched a state-wide fund drive, noting from the election results that a large number of people wanted the property preserved. Purchase of Cross Ranch was not funded by the usual handful of large donors. A few corporations contributed but the remainder of the money came in hundreds of modest gifts from individuals, small businesses, and civic groups. Bake sales and Boy Scouts collecting beer cans helped raise the Levis' asking price of $2.6 million, a million under market value.

THE AMERICAN prairie was once a sprawling engine of biomass, producing more energy than the corn or wheat that covers much of it now. Big bluestem grass was the most obvious cover, head-high when left ungrazed and wind-furrowed into waves like the sea. Soil moisture and consistency determined other members of the plant community—needlegrass, bluegrama, sedges, switchgrass, coneflowers, and wild rose. Bison, antelope, elk, deer, and periodic hordes of grasshoppers were the main grazers, their catholic tastes pruning the vegetation more evenly than today's cattle. Dry season fires periodically cleared the landscape of brush and young trees.

On today's prairie, fire is suppressed and brome grass and bluegrass are often introduced as the food preferred by cattle. Both are less resistant to drought than a mixed-grass prairie. Even in years of ample moisture the cattle trim the grass so faithfully and exclusively that noxious weeds can eventually take over unless controlled by spraying herbicides.

Sometimes, it seems, we've messed up the natural systems so badly that man has to reinvent them. On Samuel H. Ordway, Jr. Memorial Prairie Preserve near Aberdeen, South Dakota, The Nature Conservancy is trying to recreate the conditions that nurtured prairie centuries ago. A small herd of bison once again roams Ordway's 7,500 acres, land made gently lumpy by rounded piles of grass-covered glacial till. The Conservancy also scorches the land periodically with carefully controlled prairie fires, a portion at a time.

"Plants on the prairie adapted to fire, drought, and grazing," said Glen Plum, former manager of the preserve. "There's not enough of a market for bison for us to handle a large herd, so we lease to local ranchers the right to run cattle here, to generate income for the preserve and simulate the grazing once done by wild animals.

"What if there is some kind of energy revolution and we don't need the prairie for crops anymore? If none remains you've lost not only a cultural link to what made the Midwest tick, you have also lost the knowledge about how that particular ecosystem operated.

"A few years ago it was a struggle getting the right to burn. A prairie wildfire is a frightening thing, flames twenty feet high and racing with the wind, and there were people who had lost ancestors in them. But now a number of young ranchers ask how to do a burn, because they can see how healthy our prairie looks."

LEFT, BELOW:
A bison, or American buffalo, takes a dust bath on Sam Ordway Preserve. The bath sloughs off loose skin, removes burrs, and soaks up oils, leaving a thin layer of dust next to the skin that also deters biting insects.

OVERLEAF:
At home again on the range, bison graze on 7,800-acre Ordway Preserve in South Dakota. Once down to fewer than 1,000 animals from the millions that formerly roamed North America, the shaggy, herbivores now number a healthy 100,000. Conservancy research reveals that bison graze differently from the cattle that have mostly replaced them on the prairie. Cattle selectively eat fine grasses, creating a patchwork prairie eventually overtaken by less desirable plants. Bison move forward like a lawn mower, eating nearly everything and therefore maintaining a balance of prairie plants.

To teach its managers how to keep a fire from going wild, the Conservancy operates burn schools at preserves around the country. Niobrara Preserve in western Nebraska hosted one, on land big enough (54,000 acres) for numerous burns to take place. Its diverse growth, with both prairies and woodlands, provided experience for managers from around the nation.

A number of species cross paths at Niobrara, near the geographic center of the contiguous forty-eight states. Endangered piping plover and whooping cranes use the preserve's sand bars; bald eagles roost in winter on ponderosa pines, the kingly trees usually seen in the mountain west. Bluestem grass of the central prairie covers Niobrara's sandhills, but its forests contain white birch, normally associated with north woods.

In a quonset hut at preserve headquarters, students in the five-day course map strategy like battlefield commanders before taking their knowledge to the field and actually setting a fire. Students are soon tossing about terms such as flame length, ignition pattern, and optimum wind speed. Teams of a half dozen each are allotted plots of less than one hundred acres, which they will burn as a field exam. After huddling and plotting their strategy, each presents a burn plan for criticism by instructors and other students.

"Our plot appears to be about 80 acres, although only 40–60 acres of that is considered burnable," said the spokesperson for one team, after making a rough sketch of the area on a chalkboard. "We estimate the rate of spread to be 28–60 feet per minute, with back flame length of two feet and headfire flame length of 55–85 feet. Scorch height will be 40–60 feet. We will first burn black lines 30–50 feet wide around the entire plot. Our ignition pattern will be to light the area just in front of the downwind black lines first and then light the interior and burn outward . . ."

Classroom work can prepare students for the logistics of an effective burn

but not for the reality of a wall of flame roaring over hills and down ravines. "On the day of a burn I wake up with a knot of fear in my stomach," said a veteran of several prescribed prairie fires. "You know that if it ever gets away from you, politically it will be nearly impossible ever to do one again."

The prescription for fires varies and students in the field carefully check wind speed, humidity, and the height of vegetation before touching one off. "It depends on what you want to accomplish—suppress brush, kill small trees," says Mary Huffman, a fire school student who manages a small Conservancy preserve in Ohio. Her spare build and quick movements give her a look of birdlike attentiveness, accentuated by a single soprano chirp when she is amused. She is dead serious about safety in prescription burning, however, and it is not just cranky neighbors she is worried about. Back in Ohio she wants to convince some public officials to burn their parks.

When the first white settlers came to what is now Toledo they saw a very different, almost parklike kind of woodland. Huge oaks were anchored in the sandy soil, so comfortably spaced that their thick limbs spread to wide crowns. Little underbrush cluttered the ground beneath them. As one settler wrote in his journal, "You could drive a wagon off in any direction with no trouble."

The "oak openings," as they came to be called, sat on an old lake bed, formed when the last glacier dammed up the Niagara River and flooded the area. When the glacier finally receded and the lake drained, wind sculpted a rolling landscape of sand. Oak savannahs grew on the higher, dry soil, and the swales between the dunes became soggy sedge meadows. Both levels contained a high level of genetic diversity, including plant species found nowhere else in the region.

The unique open woodlands were maintained by frequent fires set by native Americans for reasons that are not yet clear, perhaps to attract browsing

game, perhaps to promote berry growth, perhaps—for fun. One early visitor to a native village recorded that the Indians set the forest floor ablaze seemingly to entertain their guests, as in, let's go sit on the big dune and watch the nice fire.

Fires and soggy marshes were not in the plans of the white settlers who replaced the Indians in the 19th century. They drained the fertile swales for farmland and either cut the big oaks or let them grow crowded with undergrowth and young trees.

In 1972 The Nature Conservancy bought 102 acres not far from the Toledo airport. It was a sad remnant of oak openings, its low swales cut through with drainage ditches and its few large trees crowded by saplings. Not far away, however, were some 4,000 acres of undeveloped land in the Toledo Metropark system, prime for restoration.

To the little Kitty Todd Preserve, named after a deceased Ohio conservationist, Mary Huffman brought her newfound burning skills and a missionary zeal to show that fire could be a tool in recreating an ecosystem. She blocked the drainage ditches so the sedge meadows could recover and she conducted a few small burns, inviting park personnel to participate. She bossed the burns, and park workers contributed radios to coordinate the effort.

"Seeds from plants that were here in earlier times lie dormant in the ground for years," said Mary, "just waiting for the right conditions to come back. After a burning we get a blush of blooming orchids." She points out a sessile tick-trefoil, rare in the state, and a globally threatened Kalms St. Johnswort.

Convinced by the results, Toledo Metroparks has now tried a few tentative controlled burns of its own, supervised by the diminutive TNC manager. In a few park locations exist the nearest thing to the oak openings of centuries ago—black oaks, white oaks, pin oaks, some with trunks six feet in diameter

ABOVE:
The sticky petals of the royal catchfly plants at Bigelow Cemetery in Ohio detain insects. But unlike carnivorous plants such as the Venus flytrap, this flower does not digest them as protein. The stickiness may ward off insects that lay eggs and produce larvae that injure the plant.

OPPOSITE:
Where pioneers rest, part of their prairie survives in lightly tended cemeteries. Conservancy biologists have found rare prairie plant species in family plots such as the Bigelow Cemetery in Ohio, uncultivated and undeveloped over the decades. Conservation easements—agreements with landowners that sites will not be disturbed—can help ensure survival of remnant species.

and so well dispersed that one could still drive a wagon between them.

"Mary works on a higher scientific plane than we do, and she can try things that we cannot because she doesn't have to answer to the public," admitted a park official. "We want to determine what these woods were like originally, and then we have to convince the public to let us use public money to restore them to that condition. Mary and the Conservancy are helping us do that."

WHEN ONE talks about altering life in a natural landscape, no better example exists than in Hawaii. When one talks about species that have developed special adaptations and might therefore be invaluable when crossbred elsewhere, Hawaii's name comes up again. America's fiftieth state, the sea-washed collection of islands in the Pacific, is a well-known mecca for tourists but it is probably much more important as a biological laboratory for evolution.

Anything that drifted, blew, or flew across the water to these volcanic tips—perhaps the most isolated land on earth—came to stay. With almost no chance of returning from whence they came to interbreed with others of their kind, wild immigrants to Hawaii became models of variation and specialization over thousands of years. The best example is the Hawaiian honeycreeper, a bright-colored bird that evolved into at least fifty-seven variations of one original species. To demonstrate the extent of this diversity it should be noted that in the Galapagos Islands off the coast of Ecuador, Charles Darwin marveled at finding twelve different finches evolved from a common ancestor.

While flora and fauna from South America dominate the Galapagos, those in Hawaii originate from around the globe. No large predators or plant-eaters made the swim, so Hawaiian plants and animals gradually gave up their defenses. Mint lost the strong scent that in other areas protected it against grazers, raspberries lost their thorns, and a number of birds quit flying for lack of need.

OPPOSITE:
Sugar cane's green geometry has replaced many of the unique endemic species in Hawaii. By 1800 nearly eighty percent of the islands' original lowland habitat had been severely altered, including the loss of plant and animal species found nowhere else in the world. Conservancy programs now attempt to preserve the species that remain.

How important is species variation? In practical terms, two immediate examples come to mind. A miller moth found in Hawaii was crossed with the cotton-eating boll worm, producing sterile male offspring. Released in cotton country on the mainland where they mate uselessly with females, the sterile males can reduce crop-ruining infestations without the use of pesticides. The nectarless Hawaiian cotton plant lends a further weapon to biological insect control: crossed with commercial cotton it eliminates the sweet nectar that attracts aphids, again avoiding the use of pesticides.

What forces have been at work in threatening Hawaiian species? In 1970 on the island of Molokai an amateur naturalist named Joan Aidem found the remains of an extinct flightless goose. The leg bones were thick as a deer's, but the wings were mere flippers that wouldn't have launched a pigeon, leaving the large bird easy prey to the first Hawaiians. The goose was cooked. Extinctions of species accelerated rapidly with the coming of Europeans, whose ships brought cattle to feed the new settlers, exotic plants for the same reason, and rats, who hitchhiked in the holds. The cattle trampled and grazed into oblivion plants found only in Hawaii, and the new flora crowded out natives that had existed for millennia. Rats ate bird eggs and nestlings, and then, mongooses that were brought in to control the rats ended up feasting on birds as well. The Hawaiian crow, once the royal bird of the islands, now numbers less than a dozen; it is believed that only three are living in the wild.

Hawaii accounts for only two-tenths of one percent of the entire U.S. land mass but has more than a fourth of the nation's endangered species. Worldwide, a third of all species of birds lost in recent decades were wiped out in Hawaii. Entire ecosystems are threatened as well; out of 150 different communities of plants and animals, more than half will be lost in the next twenty years unless action is taken.

ABOVE:
The last natural beach in Hawaii, Mo'omomi Dunes is home to an endemic ground-hugging daisy called liphochaeta, *here carefully palmed by TNC refuge manager Ed Misaki. Construction, livestock grazing, and dune buggies have altered all other Hawaiian seashores. Several plant species not found elsewhere still grow on unblemished Mo'omomi, now protected by The Nature Conservancy.*

OPPOSITE:
Fading sun lights the Mo'omomi dunes on Molokai, Hawaii.

All but flightless, nene geese of Hawaii get above the clouds by walking on the ridges of Hawaii's island of Maui. Lacking predators, other Hawaiian birds completely lost their ability to fly over the centuries, but were wiped out by the first human residents. In addition, escaped pigs and goats of earlier Hawaiians destroy the brushy highlands that serve as a sponge and filter for island freshwater supplies. By buying some properties and managing others, the Conservancy restores habitats so that both unique Hawaiian species and valuable watersheds can survive.

Green Hawaii's rain forests are being denuded by pigs and goats gone wild and by axis deer, which were brought in for sport. The deer and goats eat foliage down to the bare earth, and the pigs root the ground into furrows that quickly erode. The west side of Haleakala Mountain on the island of Maui is a prime example, a former rain forest now gullied and covered only with short grass. Fresh water is lost along with the soil. The former mat of rain forest vegetation allowed rainwater to soak into the earth and emerge further down-hill as springs and clear streams. Now it rushes unimpeded down the steep slopes, carrying the mountainside with it into the sea.

"In my lifetime we used to·hunt goats up there and you had to push through the brush," said Peter Baldwin, president of century-old Haleakala Ranch, which is spread over 30,000 acres of the mountain. On lower slopes,

6,000 head of beef cattle graze and 2,000 acres have been leased to a dairy operation.

"We knew all along that the loss of vegetation affected the watershed, but I wasn't aware at first of the importance of retaining birds and plants because of their uniqueness."

The east side of the mountain is still forested, although feral goats and pigs spilling over the ridge threaten to denude it as well. In the mid-1980s the company gave The Nature Conservancy the right to manage the physical environment on Haleakala Ranch. To remove the unwanted animals the Conservancy built miles of fence, partitioning the forest into a series of large lots. Within those confines the feral stock can be eliminated by designated hunters.

Fence-making is one of ranching's more odious jobs. Through a jungle on the steep side of a mountain it is a stockman's nightmare. At Haleakala a three-foot-wide path must be hacked out of seemingly impenetrable ferns, vines, and thornless but thick wild raspberry. Roots and rock resist the metal fenceposts pounded into the ground to hold up the 39-inch hog wire fence, which must be tight enough to hold in pigs, but loose enough so fallen trees don't snap it. Rain falls for days at a time. Construction averages a mile a month.

Eradication of feral animals is underway on the island of Molokai as well, not always to enthusiastic public support. Some Hawaiians on Molokai still rely on gardens, fishing, and pigs they hunt in the forests for sustenance. They objected when the Conservancy began hunting down wild porkers as part of their management plan for TNC's Kamakou Preserve. A fellow Hawaiian, Ed Misaki, young TNC manager of Kamakou, saw his neighbors using the forest without understanding how it worked, how important the tangle of plants was to the slow, water-filtering process. In public meetings and education programs he now tries to turn their attitudes around.

All Hawaii is targeted for outdoor enlightenment. An Awareness Campaign aims at informing legislators and other top officials about environmental issues. To buy more time for Hawaii's beleagured species, the Conservancy's Islands of Life campaign aims at raising ten million dollars, one of the largest fund drives in the history of the islands.

"Ninety percent of Hawaiian culture is connected to its plants," said Rennie Silva, grounds manager at the Maui Zoo and Botanical Gardens. "Hawaiians made their canoes from trees, leis from flowers, clothing from grass, medicine from plants, clubs and fishnets from vegetation. The hula was a way of talking about people's relationship with nature. People have to become aware of that relationship again."

And not just in Hawaii.

CHAPTER THREE

The Business of Saving Species

Panther Ranch in southwest Texas enjoyed a fleeting fame. At 67,000 acres it was for a short time the largest privately held preserve in the world.

The baked, scrubby Chihuahuan desert seemed an unlikely candidate for distinction. Ranching had brought a familiar story of overgrazing and too much hunting. The stubborn grasses in the parched soil had been reduced to an uncertain mosaic against a background of gray, eroding rain-packed dirt called hardpan. When the Harte family donated the ranch to a delighted Nature Conservancy in 1984, Texas businessman Houston Harte indicated that he was happy to make the gift, but chagrined that it was such "sorry land."

Sorry it might have been, but in the eyes of the Conservancy, worth saving. In the ego-shrinking grandeur of Chihuahuan desert, blue-skyed and seemingly limitless in scope, live a number of species in need of protection. Mountain lions, hunted as stock-killing varmints on neighboring ranches, dwell in the rock-strewn mountains scattered through the ranch. They prey on mule deer and antelope that still graze the plains and on the tough little pigs called javelinas that thread the dry arroyos in their stiff-legged trot. A TNC survey undertaken after it acquired the property revealed two rare plants, cliff thistle and Havard penstemon.

—◆—

In 1989 the Conservancy gave most of Harte's domain away. Some 10,000 acres were first sold and the money used to buy another preserve, but the remaining 56,720 acres were deeded to the National Park Service. Panther Ranch, once the biggest private preserve in the world, became an extension of Big Bend National Park that sprawls along 118 miles of the Rio Grande.

In an era of empire-building and ego satisfaction, the low-profile posture of The Nature Conservancy can sometimes cause a mental double take. Saving species, not amassing land, has remained its primary business, but its quiet technique has a strategic as well as a philosophical purpose. Publicity and power are supposed to be good business, but the Conservancy has found the opposite.

"Many of our big donors are the kind of people who don't like the nature and extent of their contributions to be known publicly," said an officer at national headquarters. "Our quiet approach appeals to them."

"We operate through a lot of extraordinary partnerships," said another, "and to me, rule number one is that you do not upstage your partner."

The quiet approach is especially important in the West, where public land holdings are vast. "When a lot of people hear you want to buy property for a preserve they immediately think it's a federal land grab, and they begin to resist," said a TNC worker in a western office.

The techniques have been so effective that The Nature Conservancy has outperformed the federal agency entrusted with implementing the Endangered Species Act of 1973. Throughout the 1980s the Conservancy acquired more than three times the amount of conservation acreage than the United States Fish and Wildlife Service (USFW). In early 1989 a report from the General Accounting Office criticized USFW for its sluggish performance in protecting wildlife, citing the lack of a systematic, coordinated plan for halting the decline of those in danger of extinction.

Once its Heritage Program has identified species in need of protection, the Conservancy's ability to act quickly in saving habitat stems from the use of its Land Preservation Fund, a revolving pool of millions of dollars that acts as an investment bank. When the organization's state offices need to close a property deal immediately they can borrow from the fund, then pay back the amount—plus interest at the prime rate—through the slower process of raising money from members, businesses, and well-to-do individuals in a regional fund campaign.

Former TNC vice president Dave Morine, a national staff member for nearly two decades, traces the history of the Land Preservation Fund: "In 1955 the Old Dominion Foundation donated $7,500 for a loan to buy some property and they told us that what we really needed was seed money. This gave birth to the revolving fund now called the Land Preservation Fund. The Conservancy has added to it occasionally through donations to account for inflation, and it now stands at more than $130 million."

Annual dues from some 600,000 members help maintain the staff and the

A researcher spoon-feeds two attentive peregrine falcon chicks at the World Center for Birds of Prey in Idaho, largest facility of its kind. TNC funding helped establish the Center. Hatched by an artificially inseminated mother and raised in an incubator, the chicks may later be released to augment imperiled wild populations.

preserves, and a few purchases such as Cross Ranch in North Dakota have been funded as true grass roots campaigns among regional residents. But the building blocks of TNC success in saving land have been large donations from wealthy individuals, plus some hefty gifts from corporations, a source long scorned by environmental groups.

The appeal to big business began in the 1970s when the environmental and corporate worlds were at loggerheads. It seems ancient history now, in an era when political candidates embrace the Green movement and oil companies buy television time to show how they save species. But when Pat Noonan and his coterie of MBAs began asking companies to save habitat, most businessmen saw environmentalists as soft-headed hippies who in turn viewed them as evil exploiters.

"Ed Kingman was one of our earlier vice-presidents and he brought to the organization a positive attitude about people," said Dave Morine. "But in my opinion the negotiating style adopted was purely Pat Noonan, whose attitude was that nobody is ever wrong."

The donation in 1973 by the Union Camp Corporation of some 50,000 acres of Dismal Swamp, valued at $12.6 million, was a landmark of TNC success with big business. For a time it was believed to hold the record as the biggest single corporate gift in history. As an example of the Noonan technique, however, Morine remembers the bargain purchase of the second biggest chunk of the wetland straddling North Carolina and Virginia.

"Pat and I went in to see this guy named Bull Hedley, who had the demeanor to fit his name," says Morine, author of a light-hearted book called *Good Dirt: Confessions of a Conservationist.* "If he didn't exactly throw us out on our ear, it was the next thing to it.

"We're picking ourselves up, brushing off our clothes," continues Morine

with customary hyperbole, "and Pat says 'well, we made some progress.' Next thing you know he's writing him a letter, 'Dear Mr. Hedley, it was a pleasure meeting you, we too are believers in the free enterprise system and if you're ever in Washington please stop by.' He follows it up with another letter. 'Dear Mr. Hedley, here's a piece I saw the other day, a situation similar to your own . . . ' We eventually got that chunk of the swamp. Pat would just never let up, never believe the worst in anybody, never get discouraged."

Morine's puckishness is as much a trademark of the TNC troops as Noonan's optimism. "I look for a little humor in people," said a hiring officer at national headquarters. "You can get awfully tense in this business of saving land and species. You have to be able to laugh off a disappointment and not be overwhelmed by events."

Jokes and optimism don't buy property. Central to Conservancy success are the business minds that can close a land deal, entice a gift from a large donor, or devise a tax shelter to save a rare plant. Imagine the negotiating skills required when the New Jersey office convinced operators of a rest home that they should include safeguards for rattlesnake habitat. "Conservancy workers are astute business people, whose bottom line happens to be biological diversity, not money," said a Houston realtor about TNC troops he had encountered.

Since donations and bargain sales of property have played a large part in the organization's financial maintenance, TNC land acquisition personnel are well-versed in tax laws. A few years ago "bargain sales"—selling land below its market value and deducting the difference as a charitable contribution—produced both cash income and a tax deduction that could actually make the donor more money than a direct sale of the property. Tax reforms of the 1980s eliminated that difference, but benefits in donating land still exist. Tax advantages may be less, but as TNC points out to corporations, property given for

Regal resident at the Birds of
Prey Natural Area, the bald
eagle prefers areas like the
Snake River where it can soar
in search of fish. Population of
the national symbol plummeted
dangerously a quarter century
ago, due mostly to the use of
DDT, which has since been
outlawed in the U.S. Bald
eagles have been making a
comeback nationwide in recent
years.

Heavyweights of the Birds of
Prey Area, golden eagles like
this one feed on jackrabbits and
cottontails.

A juvenile red-tailed hawk
strikes a defensive posture at
the approach of intruders. The
oak tree nest is in TNC's
Chiwaukee Preserve in
Wisconsin.

environmental purposes can reap benefits in public relations as well.

If the land desired by TNC cannot be bought at any price, the next possibility might be acquiring a conservation easement. Convincing an owner to restrict use of the land to protect certain species and receive tax advantages by doing so requires a knowledge of tax laws that few people have bothered to obtain. "We've practically written the book on conservation easements," said the proud director of a state TNC chapter.

The Conservancy's land savers are also expert in knowing opportunities to tie in with government grant programs—wetlands protection money or federal funds for endangered species, for example—for help in acquiring land. Whether land is protected by purchase or easement, the result has been tens of thousands of acres on which rare species find a better chance of survival.

Understanding all the possibilities that might appeal to a reluctant landowner and knowing when to apply the right formula requires a certain amount of creativity. Convincing the landowner to accept the deal requires salesmanship. One young man who wanted to work at TNC studied for and acquired a

real estate license, then was told by TNC personnel that he was light on persuasiveness. To improve those skills he became a vacuum cleaner salesman. Re-applying with TNC he finally got the job of his dreams, acquiring land for The Nature Conservancy.

The work attracts idealistic young people who have grown up with environmental concerns but are also drawn to the complexity and power struggles of high finance. "I'm handling land deals in the millions of dollars," said a state office director in his mid-thirties, barely able to contain his delight. "I'm not making a lot of money but the salary allows my family to live comfortably. And I'm a happy individual, doing something that I think is terribly important. The Conservancy is building a genetic library for the future."

In the ideal project TNC buys the land, gets the money back through donations or resale, and in the process turns the property over to a third party qualified to manage it. It is rarely so simple. After the biologists from TNC have identified species that need protection, the strategies for saving them are often intricate and extend over years. Negotiations for the massive Gray Ranch property in New Mexico began in 1982 and the deal was completed nine years later.

A southern purchase has become a classic among TNC strategies. The Conservancy first heard in 1973 that one of the last great riverine swamps on the continent might be lost. The valuable tract of bottomland hardwoods along more than thirty miles of the Pascagoula River in Mississippi was owned by the Pascagoula Lumber Company. When some major stockholders would not accept the Conservancy's purchase offer of $15 million, TNC bought controlling interest in the company and then sold the land in 1976 to the state of Mississippi, which now operates more than 35,000 acres as a state park.

Another buyout of a company rescued more than 2,000 acres from development not far from New York City, where a threatened bird of prey was the

Conservancy worker Catherine Macdonald overlooks Warner Basin Lakes, a series of eastern Oregon waterholes important to cattlemen and conservationists alike. In 1989 the Conservancy bought 7,882 acres to protect migratory waterfowl that use the lakes and shorelines. The property was transferred to the Bureau of Land Management, which now allows only grazing that does not conflict with waterfowl use. Some 850 additional acres were purchased in 1991, part retained by the Conservancy and part transferred to the U.S. Fish and Wildlife Service as part of Harte Mountain National Antelope Refuge.

preservation target. Aeon Realty Company owned a wooded third of Shelter Island, located off the far end of Long Island, and leased it to a shooting club. One of the East Coast's largest populations of ospreys spends summers on Shelter Island, occupying nine active nests and feeding on fish in the salt marshes. A rare plant called sea-beach knotweed grows on the rocky shores.

The shooting of waterfowl made both the ospreys and the Conservancy nervous, but the realty company refused to sell the property apart from its other holdings. So TNC bought everything, including six brownstone houses in Manhattan, two warehouses in Miami, plus oil and gas leases in three states, for $10.65 million. When everything had been resold except the Shelter Island property, the outlay for what is now Mashomack Preserve totaled some five million dollars.

In summer when the year-round population of 1,800 on Shelter Island swells to 12,000, urbanites learn about life in the wild on nature walks led by preserve managers. Some deer hunting is allowed to keep that population under control, but waterfowl are no longer shot. The slower pace seems to agree with the ospreys. The nine active nests have more than doubled since the TNC purchase in 1980.

Other creative purchases now legendary in TNC annals include acquisition of a small airport on Martha's Vineyard to save a remnant of eastern grasslands, and creation of a dummy corporation to buy Virginia barrier islands from residents who wanted to see it developed. But a new level in compromise and cooperation was reached in 1984 with establishment of a 13,000-acre preserve in an area of expensive real estate at Palm Springs, California.

In the Coachella Valley, sandbox for the rich and famous, was a desert that was increasingly greened by encroaching lawns and golf courses. A native there, a tiny reptile, had made the federal endangered species list. The fringe-toed

◆———

lizard, more slender than a finger, nine inches long to the end of its stiletto tail, escapes enemies and midday heat by diving into loose sand and squirming through it—sand-swimming so to speak—to safety. The physical equipment allowing it to do this represents a marvel of adaptation: nostrils with a sand filter, overlapping eyelids that are partly transparent, fringed ear flaps, and an eyelike sensor on top its head that allows it to monitor the amount of solar radiation it receives. The toe fringes that give the lizard its name allow the reptile to "snowshoe" over loose sand before plunging beneath the surface.

Not just any sand will do. The lizard's hiding place originates in the nearby Little San Bernardino Mountains, where seasonal outwash carries minute fragments of rock into the valley. Winds on the vast plains blow it into large dunes, where fine grains slide down the sides and form pools of a liquid consistency at the bases—habitats for the sand-swimming lizard.

The U.S. Fish and Wildlife Service reasoned that these habitats, accrued over millenia, were not compatible with the houses, the green lawns, and the asphalt envisioned by the Sunrise Development Company, whose plans were

ABOVE:
Desert hi-tech: wind generators sprout between irrigation channels in Coachella Valley. Strong winds that sweep the desert also build the dunes where fringe-toed lizards dwell.

RIGHT:
Seemingly inhospitable to life, the powdery sand dunes of California's Coachella Valley offer sanctuary to many species, including especially the endangered fringe-toed lizard.

smiled upon by a development-hungry county government that anticipated higher tax rolls. Sunrise Development had a residential plan for the entire valley. Fish and Wildlife, entrusted with enforcing the Endangered Species Act, threatened to shut it all down. A classic confrontation had begun when The Nature Conservancy was asked to help negotiate a settlement between the developers, county officials, environmentalists, and USFW.

Participants now agree that the talks began with considerable hostility, but leadership overcame ill feelings. Some at Sunrise wanted to fight the issue in the courts, but president William Bone insisted on working it out and named Paul Seltzer, a lawyer with a reputation for reason and fairness, to represent the company in the talks. Biologist William Mayhew of the University of California, who first warned of the lizard's loss of habitat, stressed the importance of retaining open spaces for the future, "like New York's Central Park."

"That appealed to me," said outspoken Corky Larson, who participated in negotiations as county supervisor from nearby Riverside, California. "Personally I thought they were overdoing the business of saving this little lizard. But I liked the idea that a hundred years from now people would be glad we saved open space and the wildlife that was in it. The Nature Conservancy played a super role in fund-raising, negotiating with property owners, suggesting deals. The cooperation was so exciting."

What followed was a model of compromise and a hallmark of the Conservancy's ability to work with business, environmental, and governmental interests. "We're not against development," said former TNC chairman David Harrison in summing up the Coachella agreement. "We know if you stick a thumb in the dike against development in one place it's going to pop up elsewhere. So the answer is alternative development to protect biotic diversity."

A consulting firm assessed the land wanted for the preserve and said that

$25 million would be required to buy it and manage it in perpetuity. The Richard King Mellon Foundation, an important player in several Conservancy land deals, got the ball rolling with a $2 million no-interest loan that allowed TNC to acquire an option on land for a preserve. The money was later paid back through a fund drive in the Palm Springs area. Other money came from federal government allocations for preserving endangered species, from the State of California, the McCallum Foundation, and from mitigation fees paid by Sunrise for land outside the preserve that it was allowed to develop.

"Everybody got something, and gave up something," said one of the participants in the negotiations. "The environmentalists got their preserve but not as big as they wanted; Sunrise got to develop, but not as much as they wanted; the feds upheld the Endangered Species Act, but it cost them some money. And people who want to live in the area can't build as freely, but when they do, the retention of open space makes their property more valuable."

The Coachella Valley Preserve totals 13,000 acres and it adjoins a state park of 4,000 acres. The preserve itself reverted to federal ownership, but it is managed by the Conservancy.

Cooperation with the federal government in another arena gave TNC a hand in preserving habitat without buying a single acre. In 1988 the Department of Defense agreed to allow the organization to identify, document, and maintain biological diversity on more than 900 DOD installations across the country, totaling some twenty-five million acres, roughly the size of Kentucky. Most of the land is clustered in remote, unpopulated areas, and although some activities take place on them, protection of imperiled habitats is expected to result from the agreement.

Partnerships lie at the heart of the Conservancy's operation. The Natural Heritage Programs in all fifty states depend on working with state governments in cataloguing species. In 1989 TNC teamed with the huge waterfowl-preserving organization, Ducks Unlimited, to save wetlands. The first joint project involved spending $3.5 million for California farmlands and restoring them to habitat for migratory waterfowl.

A growing international program has extended into more than a dozen Latin American countries plus Canada and several island nations in the Pacific. The partnerships in these far-flung areas are with environmental organizations within the country, to which the Conservancy serves as advisor and financier. BIOMA in Venezuela was strengthened after its director, Aldemaro Romero, trained for a year at Conservancy headquarters. ANCON already existed in Panama when the Conservancy began augmenting its conservation efforts with training, technical advice, and funding.

On a much smaller scale, partnerships with individuals help save species and unique plant communities when purchase of the land is not necessary or possible. The careful language of conservation easements can legally forbid activities that would harm a species slated for protection.

Less formal than a conservation easement is the Conservancy's registry program. When the biologists identify a unique or outstanding biotic community, TNC field workers inform the landowners and seek their cooperation in protecting it. The protectors are given a plaque identifying the site as a natural areas registry and are asked to inform the organization about any threats to the area, from pollution, rights-of-way, or possible change in ownership. A biologist may stop by once a year to check on the health of the protected community. TNC field workers generally find landowners cooperative. "In most cases, when you tell someone they have something special on their land they're proud of it, and want to protect it," said a biologist in New Jersey.

From corporate donor to registry holder, the ennobling process of saving

OVERLEAF:
Sandhill cranes dot the free-spirited Platte, a wide and shallow stream that picks its way through the plains. Wet meadows along its banks are important to feeding sandhills and whoopers. Upstream impoundments now tame the spring floods and curb massive ice flows that once scoured vegetation from island hangouts. Conservancy workers now clean off trees and brush with chain saws and fire to recreate the open habitat the cranes prefer so that they can see predators.

life has been a catalyst for generosity. "You can talk about tax benefits and good publicity and sure, that's part of the reason why we get results," said a western attorney working for the Conservancy. "But altruism plays a big part too. Saving land, keeping areas natural makes people feel good."

Herman Murrah never donated an acre, yet he was instrumental in bringing TNC to Mississippi's Pascagoula River and in causing the eventual buyout of the lumber company that owned it. A self-styled "swamp rat," the slow-talking Herman was born in a small house along the river and, like his father, hunted and fished and ran a fishing camp for income. When the Pascagoula Lumber Company began talking of selling the land for timber, he whispered warnings in the ear of one of its young stockholders who shared his love of the swamp. The young man was then instrumental in bringing TNC into the negotiations that turned the area into a state park.

Now a state game warden in the park, the slow-talking Herman prowls the woods from dawn to dusk, a willing slave to maintenance and protection of nearly 20,000 acres of the park. Repairing more than one hundred miles of service roads, cultivating deer browse, nabbing poachers, and building boat ramps for park users round out his seven-day work week, although he dutifully fills out a time card for forty hours.

"I've never taken a vacation, have no plans to retire," said Herman, in his mid-fifties, sitting quietly in his pickup beside a bayou as a water mocassin zig-zagged away and a bright, attentive pair of wood ducks glided by to inspect the intruder. A yellow blotch sawback turtle, found only in the Pascagoula River basin, hauled out on a water-logged stump.

"I'm as happy as a man can be," he drawled, pouring another cup of coffee from his ever-present thermos. "Knowing I had a hand in saving this swamp is just the greatest feeling in the world."

OPPOSITE, ABOVE: *High flyers, sandhill cranes in migration often reach such altitudes that they cannot be seen from the ground.*

OPPOSITE, BELOW: *Anchored in shallows of the Platte River, sandhill cranes rest in Nebraska on their way to northern breeding grounds. More than three quarters of the migrating big waders fatten up on leftover grain in fields along eighty miles of the Platte before continuing their journey to Canada and Alaska. To secure this necessary migration stopover, some 10,000 acres along the river are now protected. Cooperating in the efforts are U.S. Fish and Wildlife, Audubon Society, TNC, and the Whooping Crane Trust, since the endangered whoopers often fly with sandhills. Land purchases total some 8,000 acres, nearly 1,200 belonging to the Conservancy.*

Blueprints for Future Landscapes

The year is 2042 and another 50-mile-wide Biosphere Reserve Corridor (BRC), from Bukavu to Tripoli, is nearing approval. The governments of Zaire, Chad, and Libya have agreed in principle to restrictions on human activity within the strip. The Environmental Planning Program (formerly the World Bank) has indicated that it will help relocate some farmers in central Chad, where cropping interferes with the savannah that continues to expand due to heavy rains. Fruit and latex gatherers in the Ituri will continue to be monitored to assure a low impact on the rain forest, and reforestation will begin in southern Libya when research is more advanced into the woodlands that existed there in the Holocene epoch some 7,000 years ago.

The Nature Conservancy office in Kinshasa points out that the new BRC is especially important because it protects the last significant herd of elephants in the wild, perhaps seventy-five. Like the twenty-three other Biosphere Reserve Corridors around the world it also allows the northern migration of animals, plants, and ecosystems as global warming nears the nine degrees of maximum change predicted by scientists in the past century.

The above scenario could unfold as both climate and environmental priorities undergo change. The Nature Conservancy turned forty in 1991, an age, as in human life

spans, when one should be vigorously realizing potential. Little more than a discussion group when it changed its name from The Ecologists Union to The Nature Conservancy in 1951, TNC has quietly grown into one of the largest environmental organizations in the U.S. Other groups still chafe over its chumminess with industry and its refusal to confront and protest environmental despoilers. Outside Magazine rated twenty-five major environmental organizations according to their "toughness" and ranked the Conservancy in a tie for last place, calling it "The pin-striped real estate broker of the environmental movement." But TNC accomplishments are noted: "They've really led the way in protecting biotic diversity," said an officer in World Wildlife Fund. And memberships continue to grow.

National Wildlife Federation and World Wildlife Fund claim more members than TNC's 600,000, but the Conservancy's financial lead is substantial. Income in 1989 totaled $168 million, more than twice that of NWF and quadruple that of WWF. With total assets of nearly $620 million its closest competitor is NWF at $48 million. No other organization can approach the five and a half million acres of habitat TNC has managed to protect, including a million-plus acres under its own management.

For all its accomplishments the organization remains a relative unknown. In a recent poll asking the general public to name the five best-known environmental groups, The Nature Conservancy came up only seventeen percent of the time. In a follow-up question—name the one most successful in land acquisition—the organization that has outperformed even the federal government improved its recognition by only one percentage point.

Although a low profile once helped them deal with large donors who associated environmentalists with radicalism, Conservancy officers now feel more visibility would be useful in the decade of environmental chic. "We'd like

to be better known," said one, "but we don't want to put money into public relations that could be put into conservation."

And more money will be needed as conservation grows more costly. Already, changes in income tax laws in the late 1980s have made land donations more difficult. Meanwhile, prices continue to climb as a more crowded planet makes property more expensive. More people and higher prices would seem to point toward smaller acquisitions. In fact, the reverse is needed, partly due to fears that the "greenhouse effect" may cause a warming of the planet.

Carbon dioxide helps makes life possible on earth by trapping infrared heat like a greenhouse. Over the past quarter century scientists measuring CO_2 content in our atmosphere have noted a steady build-up in the gas, due to the burning of fossil fuels in industry and motor vehicles. The increased CO_2 is joined by other greenhouse gases such as methane and chlorofluorocarbons (CFCs), also generated by human activities. Deforestation and rice paddies produce methane, the gas of decay. CFCs are man-made compounds used as refrigerants, foam-makers, and aerosol spray propellants. Better known as destroyers of the ozone layer, they also add to earth's greenhouse effect as they rise to the stratosphere, a journey that can take years. A number of developed countries have agreed to ban their use, but the developing world still finds them cheap and attractive.

It is difficult to argue with measurements and deny that earth's "greenhouse" is thickening. Arguments abound, on the other hand, on what effect a larger greenhouse will have on global temperatures. If the "no change" proponents lose the flip of the climate coin and earth warms up by a few degrees, the effect on species will be dramatic. Animals and plants adapted to a temperate climate will have to migrate northward. This will be especially difficult for vegetation that must leapfrog croplands and superhighways.

ABOVE:
Laelia Rubrescens *is an orchid of the dry tropics.*

OPPOSITE, ABOVE:
Winged itinerant, the scarlet-rumped tanager seen here in Costa Rica ranges north into Mexico. Many birds seen in the U.S. spend winter in Central and South America, making preservation of southern habitats as critical to feathered populations as their northern nesting grounds.

OPPOSITE, BELOW:
Long tail streaming behind it, a variegated squirrel unique to Central American dryland forests clambers over bare limbs. Most species that existed in the dry forests when Spaniards came to the New World can still be found in Guanacaste, a record sadly unmatched in forests of higher rainfall.

ABOVE:

Too cute perhaps for its own good, the white-fronted parrot often perches on the shoulders of Central American farmers, who value it as a pet. The small psittacines fly in flocks of 50–100, numbers threatened less by the pet trade than by disappearance of their mixed forest and savannah habitat.

RIGHT:

Clouds crown a hilltop at Guanacaste, a preserve for dryland species. Dry forests are even more vulnerable than wet jungles because of the easier access by logging equipment. To help Costa Rica manage its national parks, TNC raised nearly $1 million from U.S. donors and negotiated a "debt-for-nature" swap. In such agreements a donor buys out part of a country's foreign debt at a low rate and in exchange the debt-reduced nation sets aside funds for conservation.

LEFT:
Would you touch this creature? Many birds decline after what they first see as a meal flips over and looks like a small deadly snake, complete with spots that seem to be light reflecting from the false eye markings. The ingenious fakery of the viper-mimic caterpillar accentuates the rich repository of adaptations found in the threatened forests of Central America.

BELOW:
The rabbit-sized agouti, prey for jaguars, ocelots, boa constrictors, and Central American villagers, is surprised harmlessly this time by the camera flash at La Selva.

OPPOSITE,
ABOVE LEFT:
An assassin bug mimics an ant in Costa Rica, a ruse that may aid it in approaching prey or warding off predators that avoid bitter-tasting ants. The sharp appendage folded under its head serves both as a dagger and straw for sucking nutrients from its impaled victims.

OPPOSITE,
ABOVE RIGHT:
With scissor-like mandibles a leaf-cutter ant detaches a portion of leaf for transport to the colony stockpile.

OPPOSITE, BELOW:
Green sails on the forest floor: Leaf-cutter ants hold their produce aloft while trotting it home for a later food source.

A B O V E :

The squirrel cuckoo flies only as
a last resort when danger is
near. More often, it runs and
hops from branch to branch,
resembling the mammal from
which it takes its name.

O P P O S I T E :

The normally raucous magpie
jay falls temporarily silent at
Guanacaste National Park.
This member of the raven
family was named for its
resemblance to the black-tailed
magpie.

In late 1989 the Conservancy began a study of some 14,000 North American plant species to determine their vulnerability to climatic change. Each will be evaluated by some 300 TNC and state heritage botanists to determine its population, distribution, and adaptability. Those with especially low tolerance to shifts in temperature and rainfall may require special preservation techniques, such as transplanting to a more suitable location.

At the very least, present preserves must be enlarged to allow northern migration. Ideally, entire corridors left undeveloped could snake longitudinally for long distances, ribbons of biosphere reserves such as the one suggested at the beginning of this chapter. Such a program is already underway on a much smaller scale in the "greenway" activity currently sweeping the U.S.

Greenways are linear corridors left as natural as possible and connecting to other, larger natural areas. Recreation in the form of hiking and biking often sparks their designation by states, municipalities, and local land trusts, but biologists have recognized their value as wildlife passages as well. The corridors can be of any size, but due to the expense of acquiring land they tend to be narrow—abandoned railroad rights-of-way converted to trails, for example, or streams left undeveloped for a few feet on each bank. The Conservancy wants future acquisitions to be large enough to buffer protected species against human activities.

"We look at some of our earlier projects now—quarter-acre cemeteries and twenty-acre timber tracts—and realize they are becoming ecological islands that might not remain viable," said scientist Bob Jenkins. "Acquisitions are important to us and always will be. But more and more we will be arranging easements for responsible land management, working with county supervisors on zoning laws, or buying land and then selling it again with restrictions on how it can be used.

ABOVE:
Spines on the orb spider of Central America's rain forests make it a prickly meal for birds and lizards.

OPPOSITE:
Costa Rica's little dragon draws the attention of a camera-toting visitor, from a safe distance. Cornered, Iguanid ctensaour *can cause painful wounds by whipping its spiny tail, and its powerful jaws can break fingers. Locals eat the lizard, which they call* gorrobo; *researchers believe it may have valuable medicinal properties.*

The rain forest lives up to its name as a Swiss visitor to La Selva crosses a stream swollen by unusually high downpours. Behind her wades Charles Schnell, director of the Organization for Tropical Studies, a consortium of some forty universities, mostly in the U.S., that helped Costa Rica establish La Selva to promote better understanding of the tropics. Students from the participating universities attend two-month courses here, and applicants always exceed the available space.

"You take Cheyenne Bottoms in Kansas, for example, a huge wetland where forty-five per cent of the shorebirds funnel through during migration," said Bill Weeks, chief operationing officer in national headquarters. "We don't have to own it to protect that area, but we want to make sure that farming and other activity around it doesn't damage the habitat."

In the sixties and seventies, Weeks added, the Conservancy identified threatened wildlife communities and bought the core area that was in trouble. In the 1980s the organization realized that a secondary ring had to be bought as a buffer against abrupt changes in humidity and temperature, since human activity tends to create hot spots of decreased vegetation. In the nineties, he said, TNC realizes that care must be taken to provide a second ring beyond the core so that poor agricultural practices in a region don't alter the first buffer, which in turn changes the original bulls-eye of protection.

The three-ring design is part of the Man and the Biosphere strategy, the much-heralded but little-practiced activity of the United Nations UNESCO

OPPOSITE, ABOVE:
Double camouflage of the glass-wing butterfly may give it an edge on protection. One transparent wing makes it less visible, while the eyelike markings on the other may give potential enemies reason for pause.

OPPOSITE, BELOW:
Two specimens of the Cinderella moth, Prepona demophon, show the top and bottom sides of the insect's wings. The moth flashes brilliantly in flight but shows its drab side when it lands, closing its wings to blend with the dryland hues of Guanacaste and escape predators.

LEFT:
Held hostage to science, a caterpillar of the moth Periphoba areaci was hatched and studied in laboratories of Guanacaste National Forest in an effort to better understand species of the dry forests. Enlisting local cooperation in the project, founder Dan Janzen hired local workers to collect and care for specimens that have been shipped to museums and collectors around the world.

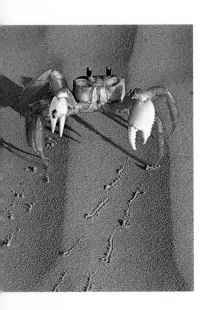

organization. The Conservancy's Virginia Coast Reserve is, in fact, registered as a UNESCO Biosphere Reserve and as such, stands as a blueprint for future projects of The Nature Conservancy.

Virginia Coast Reserve covers a stretch of classic barrier islands. Relentless wave action against the Atlantic coast builds these strips of land, nature's breakwaters. The quiet estuaries between the islands and the mainland grow rich with production of finfish and shellfish, and migrating birds pause there in fall until agreeable flying weather allows them to continue their southward journey. Sea turtles and sea-going birds nest on barrier islands, as do human vacationers whose bulky, artificial abodes often ruin the neighborhood for everyone.

Royal terns, perhaps the most sleek and graceful of the small sea birds, prefer a lonely, open stretch of sandy beach so they can nest in flocks of perhaps 1,500 birds. The Atlantic coastline has become so developed that the terns can find only three sites appropriate for nesting, one of them the huge Virginia Coast Reserve.

The first of Virginia's barrier islands was bought in 1970, and an aerial tour of that first acquisition resulted in almost serendipitous purchase of its neighbors. Donors being flown over Godwin Island looked down at the filigree of offshore land adjoining it and one of them remarked, "Why don't you just buy the rest of these?" The suggestion was backed with more money and Virginia Coast Reserve (VCR) now stretches along sixty miles of the Atlantic.

As Rhode Islander Keith Lewis observed on Block Island, coastal seawater is only as good as the shore that feeds it. Recognizing that development was inevitable, the Conservancy also bought 6,000 acres inland from the islands, with plans to guide their development in a way that won't harm the marine environment.

ABOVE:
A ghost crab, common beach species, skitters over its favorite haunt. Once an accepted predator of shorebird nests, it is now considered a threat to some bird populations since oceanfront development has upset the natural balance.

OPPOSITE:
Snowy egrets squabble at roost on Virginia Coast Reserve.

One good tern seems to deserve another, and another, and another, at a royal tern creche on Virginia Coast Reserve, the last remaining chain of undisturbed barrier islands with habitat for nesting seabirds on the East Coast. Up to 1,500 flightless chicks congregate in one creche, enabling volunteers to easily round them up for banding each spring.

A volunteer at Virginia Coast Reserve places a royal tern chick outside a wire corral after attaching to its leg a metal band with the date and location inscribed on it. Biologists want to learn more about the habits of royal terns, which have become vulnerable because they nest in dense colonies easily devastated by natural predators, or by the pets of human seashore residents.

"Norfolk is only twenty minutes away from the Chesapeake Bay bridge-tunnel that allows people to come here," said John Hall, VCR manager. "An $18 round-trip toll has slowed traffic so far, but payoff of the bridge will eliminate or reduce that toll and development will come fast."

To beat high-density housing to the punch, TNC plans development of its own on what it calls a "megasite." The 6,000 acres, divided into twelve properties, will only be sold to buyers who agree to operate their plots under certain restrictions. Any farming must include precautions against pesticides and herbicides draining into the sea. Erosion must be checked to prevent siltation of the estuaries.

"Many farmers in this area are also watermen who make extra money as commercial fishermen," said Hall. "We think they'll go along with the restrictions when they see the financial advantages. Scallops used to be an important catch here until erosion destroyed the eel grass that nurtured them."

Urban visitors may still enjoy the coast on one of the sites. Its buyers plan to capitalize on the color and romance associated with commercial fishermen by operating a small bed and breakfast hotel near a rural dock. Visitors will be able to experience all the trappings of a working fishing community, eat fresh seafood, go on nature walks, and enjoy the waterman culture in a way that would be mutually beneficial to them and the locals.

Whether by farming, tourism, or retirement homes "we want to demonstrate that human activity can take place without harming the environment," said Greg Low, director of the VCR megasite project. "We can't buy up the whole coast and determine how it will be used. But we hope the idea will catch on, that land preserved correctly will benefit the land next to it and the concept will spread from farm to farm on its own. It's a pilot project for an idea we would like to see spread over the whole country."

OPPOSITE, ABOVE:
An American oystercatcher checks its brood at a simple, open-sand nest.

OPPOSITE, BELOW:
A black skimmer, the only bird whose lower mandible is longer than its upper, hovers over its newly hatched chick.

OPPOSITE:

A visitor to Arizona's Hartwell Canyon snaps a record of the Indian pictographs protected in a 50-acre donation to the Conservancy made by a Sedona couple. In addition to gaining a tax write-off, Bob and Mary Kittredge were allowed to continue living on the property for life.

OVERLEAF:

The cliffs of Hartwell Canyon near Sedona, Arizona, were kept uncluttered by a land donation.

"Virginia Coast Reserve is absolutely critical to our future," said Bill Weeks. "What we learn and do there determines how we're going to operate for years to come. By the end of the 1990s we hope to have a hundred VCRs around the country."

And more around the world. The Conservancy's international program, started in 1974, now helps preserve land and species in more than a dozen Latin American countries and several Caribbean nations. Heritage programs in Canada are beginning to inventory species, and headquarters are being set up in Palau and Indonesia for projects in the Pacific. In mid-1990, twelve Conservation Data Centers in as many foreign countries were cataloging species and biological communities reported by field biologists, noting those of special concern that might need protection.

With two-thirds of the species on earth found in the rain forests, compared with only ten percent in North America, The Nature Conservancy will increasingly be looking abroad. A "Parks in Peril" program works with governments that have designated areas as national parks but fail to protect them. Some 275 areas in the U.S. and abroad have been targeted by TNC as potential "bioreserves" like Virginia Coast Reserve.

In the U.S., emphasis is already shifting from acquisitions—still made when possible—to partnerships in improved land use. A typical Conservancy coup in the future may be the engineering of a county-wide agreement on safe farming and manufacturing practices that protects streams and natural woodlands, rather than the purchasing of another Gray Ranch.

"One thing won't change; we'll still be in the biodiversity business," said Bob Jenkins, the scientist who helped make saving species a Nature Conservancy hallmark. "One way or another we'll do it the way we always have, by preserving areas in which species can survive."

Directory of Preserves

The following is a directory of some Nature Conservancy preserves that may be visited. Call the state field office for directions before visiting any preserve.

ALABAMA (205) 933-5133

1. Pratt's Ferry Preserve
   Bibb County, Alabama
   Special features: Alabama croton (shrub); on the Cahaba River

2. DeSoto Woods
   Fort Payne, Alabama
   Special features: stand of old oak trees

ALASKA (907) 276-3133

1. Palmer Hay Flats State Game Refuge
   (Co-op with the State Game Department)
   Palmer, Alaska (north of Anchorage)
   Special features: salmon and moose migrations

ARIZONA (602) 622-3861

1. Hassayampa River Preserve
   Wickenberg, Arizona
   Special features: stately cottonwoods; zone tailed hawks

2. Muleshoe Cooperative Management Area
   Wilcox, Arizona
   Special features: upland desert cacti; sycamore forests

ARKANSAS (501) 372-2750

1. Lorance Creek Natural Area
   Little Rock, Arkansas
   Special features: hardhack spiraea; *Nyssa biflora*

2. Rock Island Railroad Prairie
   (Co-owned with the Arkansas Natural Heritage Commission)
   Hazen, Arkansas
   Special features: Oenothera sessilis; sand cherry

CALIFORNIA (415) 777-0487

1. Santa Cruz Island
   Off the coast of Santa Barbara, California
   Special features: Santa Cruz Island fox; Santa Cruz Island ironwood

2. Cosumnes River Preserve
   Galt, California
   Special features: valley oak riparian forest; sandhill cranes

COLORADO (303) 444-2950

1. Phantom Canyon
   Livermore, Colorado
   Special features: Laramer laetes; on north fork of Cache la Poudre River

2. San Miguel River Preserves (three preserves)
   Stretching forty miles from Uravon to Ophir, Colorado
   Special features: three different riparian forest plant communities

CONNECTICUT (203) 344-0716

1. Devil's Den
   Weston, Connecticut
   Special features: bobcats; worm-eating warblers

2. Rock Spring
   Scotland, Connecticut
   Special features: bald eagles; worm-eating warblers; canoeing

DAKOTAS (701) 222-8464

1. Cross Ranch
   Hensler, North Dakota
   Special features: bison; bald eagles

2. Samuel H. Ordway Jr., Memorial Preserve
   Leola, South Dakota
   Special features: bison; pintail ducks

DELAWARE (302) 739-5700

1. Hill Preserve
   Middleford, Delaware
   Special features: Atlantic white cedar; borders Nanticoke River

2. Still Pond Preserve
   Lewes, Delaware
   Special features: tiger salamander; Carolina bay

FLORIDA (407) 628-5887

1. Blowing Rocks Preserve
   Tequesta, Florida
   Special features: barrier island; sea turtles

2. Tiger Creek Preserve
   Babson Park, Florida
   Special features: Florida scrub jay; scrub plum

GEORGIA (404) 873-6946

1. Marshall Forest
   Rome, Georgia
   Special features: old growth forest

2. Charles Harold Preserve
   Metter, Georgia
   Special features: Georgia plume; longleaf pine

HAWAII (808) 537-4508

1. Kamakou
   Island of Molakai
   Special features: rainforest preserve with forest birds and 200 indigenous plants

2. Waikamoi
   Island of Maui, adjacent to Haleakala National Park
   Special features: crested honeycreeper; Maui parrot bill

IDAHO (208) 726-3007

1. Silver Creek Preserve
   Picabo, Idaho
   Special features: Great horned owl; rainbow trout

2. Thousand Springs Preserve
   Hagerman, Idaho
   Special features: crystal clear waterfalls; abundant wintering waterfowl

ILLINOIS (312) 346-8166

1. Nachusa Grasslands
   Franklin Grove, Illinois
   Special features: rocky bluffs prairie preserve; rare prairie butterflies

2. Cache River Preserve
   Bellkack, Illinois
   Special features: bald cypress trees; wood ducks

INDIANA (317) 923-7547

1. Spicer Lake
   New Carlisle, Indiana
   Special features: winterberry; button bush

2. Pine Hills Nature Preserve
   Crawfordsville, Indiana
   Special features: eastern hemlock; Canada yew

IOWA (515) 244-5044

1. Freda Haffner Preserve
   Milford, Iowa
   Special features: small white lady's slipper; prairie moonwort fern

2. Cedar Hill Sand Prairie
   Waterloo, Iowa
   Special features: cotton grass; bog willow

KANSAS (913) 272-5115

1. Konza Prairie
   Manhattan, Kansas
   Special features: tall grass prairie; prairie chickens

2. Cheyenne Bottoms
   Great Bend, Kansas
   Special features: whooping crane; least tern

KENTUCKY (606) 259-9655

1. Bad Branch Nature Preserve
   Letcher County, Kentucky
   Special features: painted trillium; brook saxifrage

2. Mantle Rock Nature Preserve
   Livingston County, Kentucky
   Special features: sandstone glade barren Communities; prickly pear cactus

LOUISIANA (504) 338-1040

1. Little Pecan Island
   Cameron, Louisiana
   Special features: migratory bird stopover

2. Tunica Hills Preserve
   St. Francisville, Louisiana
   Special features: loess hills hardwood forest; worm-eating warbler

MAINE (207) 729-5181

1. Great Wass Island
   Beals, Maine
   Special features: jack pine forest; bald eagles

2. Kennebunk Plains
   Kennebunk, Maine
   Special features: upland sandpiper; grasshopper sparrows

MARYLAND (301) 656-8673

1. Nassawango Creek Preserve
   Snow Hill, Maryland
   Special features: bald cypress swamp; prothonotary warbler

2. Cranesville Swamp
   Sang Run, Maryland
   Special features: periglacial peat bog; saw whet owls

MASSACHUSETTS (617) 423-2545

1. Schenob Brook Wetland Preserve
   Sheffield, Massachusetts
   Special features: swamp birch; hoary willow

2. Katama Plains Nature Preserve
   Edgartown, Massachusetts
   Special features: sandplain blue-eyed grass; northern harrier

MICHIGAN (517) 332-1741

1. Ross Preserve
   Covert, Michigan
   Special features: hooded warbler; blackburnian warbler

2. Pointe Betsie
   Frankfurt, Michigan
   Special features: pitcher's thistle; balsam fir

MINNESOTA (612) 379-2134

1. Blue Stem Prairie
   Glyndon, Minnesota
   Special features: prairie chickens; rare prairie butterflies

2. Weaver Dunes Preserve
   Weaver, Minnesota
   Special features: fame-flower; Blanding's turtle

MISSISSIPPI (601) 355-5357

1. Sweetbay Bogs
   Stone County, Mississippi
   Special features: large-leafed grass of Parnassus

2. Clark Creek Natural Area
   Woodville, Mississippi
   Special features: Louisiana black bear; over 40 waterfalls

MISSOURI (314) 342-0282

1. Victoria Glade
   Hillsborough, Missouri
   Special features: Freemont's leather flower; glade community

2. Trice Dedman Woods
   Plattsburg, Missouri
   Special features: old growth oak woodland

MONTANA (406) 443-0303

1. Pine Butte Swamp Preserve
   Choteau, Montana
   Special features: grizzly bears; rare plant communities

2. Crown Butte Preserve
   Simms, Montana
   Special features: pristine foothills grassland; prairie falcons

NEBRASKA (402) 342-0282

1. Niobrara Valley Preserve
   Johnstown, Nebraska
   Special features: wild turkeys; pronghorn antelope

2. Willa Cather Memorial Prairie
   Red Cloud, Nebraska
   Special features: prairie chickens; upland sandpipers

NEVADA (801) 531-0999

1. Ash Meadows—Co-op with the U.S. Fish & Wildlife Service
   Las Vegas, Nevada
   Special features: Devil's pupfish; ash meadow's blazing star

2. Stillwater Wildlife Management Area—Co-op with the U.S. Fish & Wildlife Service
   Fallon, Nevada
   Special features: great white pelican; black-faced ibis

NEW HAMPSHIRE (603) 224-5853

1. The Green Hills
   North Conway, New Hampshire
   Special features: silvering; Appalachian sandwort

2. West Branch Pine Barrens
   Madison, New Hampshire
   Special features: pitch pine; rare moths

NEW JERSEY (908) 439-3007

1. William D. & Jane C. Blair, Jr. Cape May Migratory Bird Refuge
   Lower Township, New Jersey
   Special features: least terns; piping plovers

2. Bennett Bogs Preserve
   Lower Township, New Jersey
   Special features: rattlesnake master (plant); vernal ponds

NEW MEXICO (505) 988-3867

1. Dripping Springs
   Las Cruces, New Mexico
   Special features: nine endemic plants

2. Gray Ranch
   [call the ranch directly at (505) 548-2225]
   Animas, New Mexico
   Special features: high quality grasslands; Animas Mountains ridge-nosed rattlesnake

NEW YORK (518) 869-6959

1. Mashomack Preserve
   Shelter Island, New York
   Special features: osprey; piping plovers

2. Butler Sanctuary
   Bedford, New York
   Special features: hawk watch in fall includes red-shouldered and red-tailed

NORTH CAROLINA (919) 967-7007

1. Nags Head Woods
   Kill Devil Hills, North Carolina
   Special features: maritime swamp forest; maritime deciduous forests

2. The Black River
   Wilmington, North Carolina
   Special features: old growth bald cypress swamp; Cape Fear spike

OHIO (614) 486-4194

1. Herrick Fen
   Kent, Ohio
   Special features: tamarack trees; shrubby cinquefoil

2. Brownslake Bog
   Wooster, Ohio
   Special features: pitcher plant; poison sumac

OKLAHOMA (918) 585-1117

1. Tall Grass Prairie
   Pawhuska, Oklahoma
   Special features: tall grass ecosystem; prairie mole cricket

2. Redbud Valley
   Catoosa, Oklahoma
   Special features: Dutchman's breeches; sugar maples

OREGON (503) 228-3153

1. Tom McCall Preserve at Rowena
   Hood river and the Dalles, Oregon
   Special features: Columbia river gorge endemic plant species, rare grassland community

2. Lower Table Rock Preserve
   (managed with the Bureau of Land Management)
   Jackson County, Oregon
   Special features: striped whipsnakes, bluegray gnatcatcher

PENNSYLVANIA (215) 963-1400

1. Tannersville Cranberry Bog
   Tannersville, Pennsylvania
   Special features: glacial bog; bog turtles

2. Goat Hill Serpentine Barrens
   West Nottingham, Pennsylvania
   Special features: serpentine aster (flower); serpentine chickweed

RHODE ISLAND (401) 331-7110

1. Block Island Bioreserve
   Block Island, Rhode Island
   Special features: northern harrier; barn owl

2. Goose Wing Beach
   Little Compton, Rhode Island
   Special features: piping plovers; least tern

SOUTH CAROLINA (803) 254-9049

1. Peach Tree Rock Preserve
   Lexington County, South Carolina
   Special features: longleaf pine; woody goldenrod

2. Washo Preserve
   Charleston County, South Carolina
   Special features: wading bird rookery; red-cockaded woodpeckers

TENNESSEE (615) 242-1787

1. Barnett's Woods
   Woodlawn, Tennessee
   Special features: Price's potato bean; lesser ladies tresses

2. Wash Morgan Hollow
   Jackson County, Tennessee
   Special features: floristically rich, sheltered ravine

TEXAS (512) 224-8774

1. Dolan Falls Ranch
   Del Rio, Texas
   Special features: black-capped vireo; Concho's pupfish

2. Roy E. Larson Sandylands Sanctuary
   Silsbee, Texas
   Special features: longleaf pine savannah; Texas trailing phlox

UTAH (801) 531-0999

1. Scott M. Matheson Wetlands Preserve
   Moab, Utah
   Special features: peregrine falcons; bald eagles

2. Layton Marsh Preserve
   Salt Lake City, Utah
   Special features: waterfowl, shorebirds

VERMONT (802) 229-4425

1. Chickering Bog
   Calais, Vermont
   Special features: quaking bog; twelve different rare orchids

2. Williams' Woods
   Charlotte, Vermont
   Special features: old growth oaks, ash

VIRGINIA (804) 295-6106

1. Falls Ridge
   Blacksburg, Virginia
   Special features: Addison's leatherflower; bald eagle

2. Virginia Coast Reserve
   Nassawadox, Virginia
   Special features: peregrine falcons; barrier islands

WASHINGTON (206) 343-4344

1. Skagit River Bald Eagle Natural Area
   Rockport, Washington
   Special features: bald eagle wintering ground

2. Yellow Island
   San Juan County, Washington
   Special features: fescue headland; bunch grass

WEST VIRGINIA (304) 345-4350

1. Ice Mountain
   Slainsville, West Virginia
   Special features: bristly rose; twin flowers (arctic flowers)

2. Brush Creek Preserve
   Camp Creek, West Virginia
   Special features: Canby's mountain lover; warblers

WISCONSIN (608) 251-8140

1. Chiwaukee Prairie
   Pleasant Prairie, Wisconsin
   Special features: white-fringed orchid; oak opening

2. Mink River Estuary
   Door County, Wisconsin
   Special features: dwarf lake iris; Cooper's hawk

WYOMING (307) 332-2971

1. Tensleep Preserve
   Tensleep, Wyoming
   Special features: Carey's penstemon; mountain lions

2. Sweetwater Preserve
   Lander, Wyoming
   Special features: meadow pussytoes; moose and antelope migration